THE JOURNEY Home

Judy Monroe

JUDY MONROE

ISBN: 978-1-7168-6853-5 (sc)
ISBN: 978-1-7168-6852-8 (e)

Library of Congress Control Number: 2020910704

Lulu Publishing Services rev. date: 06/17/2020

This book is dedicated to those who encouraged me to write this book, and to all who learn everything the hard way.

Contents

"Come on Black Boy, Wrestle that Freight"

As a baby, Dad used to get up during the night, lift me out of my crib, squeeze me and say to Mom, "Yup, her heart is still going."

I became healthier at the age of three after the doctors took out my tonsils. I remember the large over-head light, the clinic, and my father's smile before I fell asleep. I remember the twelve-year-old boy who shared my recovery room. I must have been fussing because he crawled under his covers, put out his foot, and entertained me with a toe ring that lit up when he curled his pinky toe.

At home, Mom moved her ironing board in front of her bedroom door so she could work and watch me as I recovered from surgery. She was surprised at how much energy I had. I jumped on her bed and ate scratchy Ritz crackers. It is funny what I remember from that year.

I also remember that I was small and adorable in a pink crinoline dress, all dressed up to go to the Grange. Grangers, the farmers in the area, the neighbors, met each month to discuss Grange and farming issues. That was back at a time when the federal government listened first to the National Grange for recommendations. Farmers were empowered then. Farmers had produced the food that fed the American troops during World War II.

My mother always laid out what my father would wear to the Grange, to church, to the "town" of Sand Lake, population 164. Once, he came into the house from the barn wearing a filthy pair of overalls with a hole in the knee. He was headed to Sand Lake to buy feed for the young stock. She said, "You … are … not … going … anywhere … looking … like … that!" He changed his clothes.

Grange meant a suit, a starched and ironed white shirt, and a pretty tie. My father was handsome with his curly dark hair and green eyes. He was strong. He was short with massive shoulders and not an ounce of fat. If something weighed two-hundred pounds and it was in his way, he picked it up and moved it. No wheelbarrow? No problem. He would put the weight on his back and crabwalk it to wherever he wanted it. Dad never weighed over one-hundred and ninety pounds.

It was Grange night and it would be well attended. Mom curled her hair and lightly touched it with sweet-smelling rose oil to make it shine. Dad wore his suit and his Fedora that was cocked just a touch to one side. He also wore a slightly arrogant, flirtatious grin.

The year was 1949 and WWII had recently ended. Our neighbors were from two groups, Baptists or Methodists. We were the only Catholic family in the community. The Baptist neighbors were a holdover from the Ku Klux Klan that had been strong in the neighborhood. SWe were safe in our community, but some of the left-over bigotry and prejudice persisted.

At the Grange, the women sat in the chairs around the right edge of the hall and the men sat on the left. During performances, the men stood at the back of the room near the walls so they could see better. As was my wont at the time, in my own happy, healthy, impish way, I was with my hero, my father. I had a cookie in my left hand and my right had a tight grip on my father's suit pant leg. I swung back and forth, back and forth, looking adorable with my blond curls, blue eyes, sweet smile and petiteness. With my pink crinoline dress, I was sure that everyone loved me. Life was secure and happy.

The entertainment started. I recognized all of my talented neighbors. It seemed that music and acting were a part of all of their lives. But we were Catholics, and everyone knew Catholics did not sing in church. We mumbled.

But this time, Grange was different. I stopped smiling and swinging, but I never let go of Dad's pant leg. What were they doing? Bales of straw had been moved in front of the low stage. Straw covered the floor. Railroad ties had been laid like tracks on the floor. Their fiddles were there, but why did my neighbors have black faces? Their heads were covered with black burlap with painted white mouths. And they smiled so funny, like a joke was coming, but I would not understand it. Their clothing was raw, brown burlap, like our potato sacks. Gunnysacks.

The music and singing started, but I was hidden behind my Dad's pant legs and holding on tight. I do not know where the cookie went, but I was no longer eating it. I was staring from between Dad's legs, a tiny hand clutching each pant leg. I did not understand that this was a black minstrel show, no blacks invited.

From the whole performance, I remember only one song, but from the age of three, I can still sing those words. My neighbors grinned, swung their arms, fiddled, kicked their feet back and forth in the loose straw, and sang, "Come on Black Boy, wrestle that freight!"

Even at the age of three it did not feel right to make fun of someone. I had never seen a black person in my life. Was I to be frightened by black people? I did not know where my fear was to be directed. My neighbors? And only if they were in dress-up? Seeing adults act this way confused me.

I do not remember more from that evening. But six years later, Mom took "us kids" to the far-off city of Grand Rapids. It was thirty miles away and a long trip for us at that time. We were on our annual fall trip to buy underwear for school from Woolworth's.

In Grand Rapids, it was a gloomy, blue-foggy day. Later I would learn that the correct word was smoggy. I had heard that busses were used in cities to pick up people and take them to someplace else. And there, an actual bus was approaching. It stopped, but it was grayer and dirtier than the air. It was picking up people. I thought, *I never want to get into anything so stinky and disgusting as that.*

Then I saw my second new thing for the day. A black man. He was running for the bus that was not waiting for him. He was a big man. He wore a neat silver-blue suit with a matching dress-up hat. Where was the burlap? He lunged for the bus that was starting to move. With his right hand, he caught the safety bar by the door and launched himself into the bus. In a fleeting moment he was gone. I stood there and wondered, is that what they meant? "Come on Black Boy, wrestle that freight."

The Way I Remember It

The family farm was located north of Grand Rapids, Michigan. People refer to the good-old days on the farm as lazy days of nostalgia. Never. Living on a farm was hard, at best. Dad and Mom and my five siblings and I, milked cows, harvested grains, raised hogs, and baled hay and straw each summer. We hoed corn rows that were so long that we made one trip across the field and back between breakfast and our noon dinner. Strawberries were picked and boiled into jam. The one-acre garden was tended every day from tilling and planting until a killing frost. We canned or froze our own meat and vegetables and everything else that Mom could cram into a Mason jar. Mom and a quart of her canned beef are comforting thoughts.

To this day, I wish our parents had chosen someplace else to live. Each day was a battle. Dad had chosen the farm because it was the farthest north that a farm could be and still have enough frost-free days to grow crops successfully. What he chose was the moraine of the Two Creeks Interstitial Glacier. This meant, our farm grew glacial rocks. Every time the soil was worked, more rocks rose to the surface. We picked the rocks out of the fields until we wore our fingerprints off our fingers. We broke steel plow points when we hit medium sized rocks. We left grooves on big rocks as our metal machinery scraped over them. Dad called the huge boulders "donnicks" that were too large to be removed from the fields. Bull dozers were used to dig deep holes beside the huge rocks. Then the machine tipped the "donnicks" into the holes and covered them. They were buried under five feet of dirt. But I swear, they clawed their way to the surface to taunt us again.

Pangborn School

My siblings and I attended a white, one-room schoolhouse, Pangborn, which means acutely distressful birth. I do not know the history of the name but it did sound ominous. We walked one mile up the big hill each morning. I remember the school, the students, and the teachers. I remember all of them by name. The one teacher had all subjects to teach and all nine grades, kindergarten through eighth. The subjects were reading, penmanship, arithmetic, geography and spelling. I liked school and I missed it during the summer. Summers were lonely.

I must have been the smallest student because I occupied the smallest desk for two years. Desk tops were smooth sanded oak with an ink well hole drilled in the upper right-hand corner. The polished wooden seats were curved to fit our butts. The seat could be tilted up or down. The filigreed iron-sided stanchions were bolted to the floor in rows of ascending size.

I was never teased about my size, or anything else. School was pleasant. But, one day when I was in the fourth grade, a girl arrived. She would join our school the next year in kindergarten. We, the twenty-eight students attending the school, crowded around Brenda to greet her. She was wearing a bright cotton, orange-gingham dress. She was tall with dark wavy hair. All of a sudden, one student called out, " Look! Brenda is taller than Judy." It was never meant to be rude. It was just an observation. I had never noticed. I was surprised that they had noticed.

Once a year, the doctor would arrive at the school. He was old and kind and dignified. His suit was black. He was small, but he sat straight in one of our little wooden chairs with his shiny stethoscope around his neck. It matched the shine in his thin, grey hair. I really liked him. I saw him checking children's ears so I spit on my finger and washed deeply into my ears. The doctor said, "That is the cleanest ear I have ever seen." I was so proud.

Morning and afternoon recesses and noon lunch were the best. As we were dismissed, we jumped up, unwrapped our sandwiches and had them eaten by the time we reached the big fire-door exit. Students leaped off the front concrete step and called, "First bat!" Each softball diamond position was called in the order of its importance and desirability. Importance meant most time with the ball, batting, pitching or running. Importance meant degree of fun. Almost every student played softball. We had never seen a basketball. I am not sure if soccer had been invented.

We loved Friday afternoons in the spring. We were excused early. Those who played softball best were loaded into the teacher's car. All bats and gloves hung out the windows. Yelling and singing could be heard as they traveled to one of the other schools for a ball game. "Jingle bells, shotgun shells, beebees all the way, Oh, what fun it is to ride in teacher's model A." Eight one-room schools participated in the softball round-robin competition.

Kindergarteners stayed for only half of the day at school and walked home for lunch. One lovely spring day, while walking home, the mailman stopped to give me a ride. I stood on the running board of his black, shiny, stubby, little car and put my arm through the open window of the door. I hung on with my elbow crooked around the metal bar between the big window and the little window, the no-draft. I was impressed by the huge pile of mail in the tiny back seat. At our mailbox, he gave me our mail. I got off the running board and scooted up the concrete steps to our house.

Spice

One cold morning, my older brother Dick, Elaine, and I were walking to school. The snow on the road had been plowed wide, past the edges of the asphalt. I saw something on the bare road. I heard the snowplow truck roaring towards us at the top of the big hill on his return trip. The sound was hitting our ears like tin in the clear zero-degree air. I recognized the thing in the road. It was my tri-colored mother cat, Spice. She was named for her three colors, salt, pepper and cinnamon. I could not understand why she did not scoot out or the way. Surely, she could hear the snowplow.

I ran to her and tried to pick her up, but she was frozen to the road. The plow was coming down the hill. I pulled on the cat. I could feel her fur being tugged. The plow was at the bottom of the hill and I ran as fast as my short legs could travel. I carried the big, long-haired cat under my right arm, back to the snow-covered stairs on the steep bank, across the yard and into the house. I placed Spice on my little wooden chair. I placed her next to the heat that rose from the furnace in the basement and through the iron grate in the floor. Her cold body continued to sit up straight up the chair seat. She looked frozen, unmoving.

Being the obedient child that I was, I ran out of the house. I would never have allowed myself to be late for school. I loved my teacher too much to be late. At the end of the day, I hurried home to see if Spice had survived. She still sat on the short chair without moving. Occasionally she shivered. She sat in the chair for two days before she began to move, but she did move. She survived for many more years and had several litters of kittens. She appeared healthy except for two inches at the tip of her tail that had been frozen, bony and hairless.

Farm Meals

I will always remember being cold. My sister and I slept in the unheated bedroom up the stairs. By January, the large window was frozen, top to bottom, an inch thick with hoar frost. The wood stove in the basement could never produce enough heat to warm the upstairs bedrooms above freezing. But, the warmest room was always the kitchen. It took large quantities of food to feed the eight of us and our mother was an incredible cook. We ate well. Mom made six pies to a time. It was never worth her time to make fewer.

Being Catholic, we observed meatless Fridays and those were Mom's most memorable winter meals. We ate at six o'clock, sharp. It could be dark and snow covered outside, but the kitchen was hot. Mom would open the oven door and let the heat escape. Every inch of the oven was filled with food, bottom to top and side to side. It tumbled out from the racks. The odor of salmon loaf, baked potatoes and huge pieces of bright orange squash in their dark green shells filled the kitchen. The broken squash chunks were brown on the edges with their own caramelized sugar. All of it steamed on our plates and was served with the fresh butter we had churned.

Our second favorite Friday winter meal was Famo buckwheat pancakes. They were eight-inch, frypan-size, thick, and dark. They were served with butter and the maple syrup that Dad had received as payment for helping a neighbor in his sugar bush in the spring. My older brother and sister and I ran and played in the snow between the trees. Buckets hung from the tapped trees, the Sugar Maples, and the sap flowed fastest on the first days when the back of winter was broken. The boiling trough was five feet long, three feet wide, and five inches deep. Dad collected each bucket from the trees. He poured the cold sap into the boiling sap in the trough. He reset the buckets and kept the fire going. He was paid with a few quarts of maple syrup, liquid amber.

Eighth Grade Graduation

I graduated from the eighth grade from Ensley Township Schools. The eighth graders had been assembled into the central school, Ensley Center, from the eight one-room schools in the district to take a placement test. The first place was taken by Donna. Everyone knew she was intelligent and would become valedictorian. As salutatorian, I was to give the speech for placing second.

On our graduation day, the sixteen graduates were brought to the tiny city of Sand Lake. I wore a pretty pink dress with crinolines and my first white, two-inch heeled shoes. I was told that everyone liked my speech because I had memorized it and had spoken loudly. I said, " We are the most worthy class ever to graduate." I felt guilty saying it. I did not see why we were more worthy than anyone else. I learned later that it was the same speech handed down to every salutatorian, year after year.

Donna and I went to separate high schools and colleges. We have greeted each other twice in the last fifty years though our homes had been only two miles apart. The evening was bitter-sweet for some in the collective class. This was the end of their education. They would not be going on to high school, or receive any formal education, ever again.

Just Pitch Rocks

A short time after graduation, I was playing softball in the neighbor's pasture field with four others. I had hit a good fly ball and was rounding third base and coming home. It would be my first chance to hit a home run, ever, but the evening was cooling down. Dew was forming on the plants. I slipped and tumbled. My left arm tangled under me and the arm broke, both bones. I looked at the arm in its strange shape and grabbed my hand. I pulled until the broken bones snapped back into alignment with each other.

It was dark and seemed late when we arrived at the family doctor's office. He took x-rays and said to Mom and Dad, "If she had broken it any worse, we would be doing surgery on her now." A thick, heavy, plaster cast was applied from the second knuckle on my hand to the pit of my arm. It was there all summer.

But, what does one do for eight weeks of summer with a useless child? I could not haul hay or hoe weeds. Needless to say, Dad would think of something. He was having a new barn built. A fortified wall, twenty feet long and two feet wide, needed to be built. It would be made of concrete and field stone. He thought it was a perfect job for me. I pitched field stone into the wall for hours and days. I used my right hand to push the heavier stones against the cast on the hand of the left arm. By the time we finished, the plaster on the hand was crushed to powder and gauze. Under the cast, my arm itched from dirt and perspiration. Only a coat hanger poked into the top of the cast offered any relief. When the cast was removed, the arm was thin, dirty and weak. After a thorough scrubbing, it was time to strengthen it and put it back to work.

Mr. Coady

I liked high school. Principal John P. Coady was my life line to a productive future. He was the first adult I had ever talked to. As children, we did not talk to adults, which included aunts, uncles, and neighbors. The older we became, the more difficult it became to talk to anyone. When would this change? Would we be able to talk to adults when we became adults? When would we start to have views of our own? Was I waiting for permission to speak?

For some reason, Mr. Coady liked my brother, Dick. He thought Dick was intelligent with "self-worth." That term seems archaic today, but it was used to express the value of someone who might "amount to a hill of beans." It seemed logical that Mr. Coady would have faith in me, too. My life would be quite different today if it had not been for him. His office door was always open to me. I walked in unannounced. I do not know why I felt welcome. After all, other students avoided the principal's office.

At the beginning of my junior year, I had grown tired of home economic classes. Also, I had become aware that I and other females were no longer a part of the mathematics classes. I stalked into Mr. Coady's office and demanded to drop home economics and add advanced algebra. He said, "Judy, I think that is a very good idea." It was a great decision. A year later, I stalked into his office and he agreed with me when I announce that I wanted to go to college, Central Michigan

University. I filled out the application form in his office. I sat in the student chair in his direct line of sight. I had not realized that the lone chair in his office was for poorly disciplined students. It was not a chair for those wishing to shed their ignorance.

Got Milk?

Milk was a big part of my life until the age of eighteen. That was when I left our dairy farm for college. I had received a scholarship and loan from Central Michigan University. I had needed that money. It was 1964, and as a successful Michigan dairy farm, our profit was $2,342 for the year. The profit was to feed and clothe a family of eight. It was not enough for one sibling to attend college.

When the television advertisement asked, "Got Milk?" my mind flooded back to our dairy farm. Dairy farmers do not just milk cows. Cows must be kept clean, sheltered, and their health must be tended. But first, they must be fed. Cattle food production starts in May when the soil is starting to warm. My father drove the tractor that pulled a three-bottom plow to the "top of the hill" and into the empty field. It took a day to plow the deep-brown, straight furrows across the length of the field. Dad would occasionally stop the tractor to pick up an Indian arrow head or remove a good-sized stone from the field. The following day, he would disc the field to smooth out the furrows. In the days that followed, he would "drill," or plant, the alfalfa seeds using the seed drill.

In the next month, a field of deep-green grass would arise and wave in the wind. By the end of June, the alfalfa could be grown to over three feet high and covered with small, pale purple blossoms. In mid-to-late June, it was time to harvest the hay. First, it was cut with a mower, and then raked into windrows. Heaven help us if it rained. The windrows would have to be re-raked and turned over to dry before the baling could begin. If cut alfalfa is rained on, it can lose thirty percent or more of its nutrients. It would not be worth feeding to large, milking Holstein cows. The hay may not be worth all of the time, gasoline, fertilizer, equipment and seed that it had cost to produce.

My sister, Elaine, was thirteen months older than I. She was the stronger and more capable daughter. By eighth grade, she was driving the tractor and was given the responsibility of baling hay. It was not an easy job. Once, when she was watching the windrow of hay being pulled into the baler, she did not see the danger above her. She drove under the low hanging branches of an apple tree and was swept off the tractor. How she missed being scooped into the baler with the hay I will never know. Somehow she escaped, climbed back onto the tractor that was still traveling and continued baling.

Each square hay bale exits the back of the baler and lands on the ground. My father was a conservative man who believed in making large bales so as not to waste the twine. A bale could weigh eighty pounds. In the seventh grade, I weighed about one hundred and ten pounds and stood 4 feet, 11 inches. Elaine was in the eighth grade and was the same size, so the bales were heavy for all of us, including my brother, Richard. We baled a total of twenty-one thousand bales of hay and three-thousand bales of straw each summer. We needed to be done with the first cutting of hay by the Fourth of July or we would spend the day hauling hay instead of going to local festivities.

The carnival was set up at the one-block square park in Sand Lake in front of St. Mary's Catholic Church. After the day's work, we wanted the rides, cotton candy and the fireworks. We liked to wander around in the dark with noisy music coming at us from all sides. Each of the six of us was given two dollars to spend, any way we wished. We would leave the fair at nine o'clock clutching something we had won that was totally useless. Rarely did we stay to see fireworks in the late evening because the cattle needed milking at 6:00 a.m. We needed to get to bed.

Every bale of hay had to be handled several times, usually six. From the ground, it was lifted onto a high wagon. Someone on the wagon piled the bales so they fit in a binding-cross pattern. Each load was piled with five tiers. If we had to use the highway to haul the hay load from one field to the barn, someone had to ride on top of the load. Someone had to lift the Ensley Center intersection street-light wire over the top of the load. If we did not do this, the wire would catch the top layer of bales and pull apart the load or pull down the stop light. People who worked at the gas station would stop their work to watch the big load of hay with the little girl on top as we traveled through the intersection. I felt so important when I was the one to ride on the top to lift the electrical wire.

The wagon load of hay was then backed uphill and into the back of the barn. Each bale was removed from the load, placed on the diagonally slanted conveyor, and carried into the haymow. From there, we piled bales until the barn was full. The mow was filled until we could not stand upright without bumping our heads on the rafters.

Hay from the fields of summer is hot, with a high internal temperature that radiates heat. The temperature in the mow would rise to over one-hundred degrees. The perspiration would drip from us until our skin dried. We had no more water to give. When the wagon was empty and before we returned to the field to get the next load, we would stop at the "horse tank." We never had a horse, but the name was a holdover from our father's days on our grandfather's farm. We would reach across the wide tank filled with water for the cows and turn on the tap. The water gushed, icy cold, from our deep well. We drank in turns from a tall, metal cup. My siblings and I still remember it as the most delicious water in the world.

During the summer, cattle would pasture in the fields. During the winter, someone would go into the haymow to "throw down hay." We would feed the entire herd of cows as they were being milked while they were standing in their stanchions. The bales were broken open and the twine was collected. It was hung on a nail between the stones of the wall so no one would trip on it. The hay was delivered in front of each cow. Sometimes we would stop and pet their warm silky noses. With all the animals in the barn at the same time, though the temperature outside could be zero, the inside was moist and warm. The breath and body heat from one sixteen-hundred-pound Holstein is impressive. The heat from the entire herd in the barn can make you sweat.

During summer vacation, as soon as the cattle were milked in the morning and breakfast was eaten, we hoed weeds out of the corn field. The rows of corn I remember most were one mile long and by the time we completed four rows, that is two at a time across the field and two back, it was dinner time. Dinner was always served at 12:36, noon time. Dad came home from the fields at exactly 12:30 every day. After dinner, he re-fueled the tractor and drove back to the field to work until supper time at six p.m. Supper was always the leftover food from noon. After supper, we headed to the barn to milk the cows a second time for the day.

There are many dangers in milking cattle. Cows are big and when they step on you or push you into a stanchion or wall, it hurts. The milking machines are metal and heavy and much heavier with thirty pounds of milk in them. I was never big or strong enough to milk the cattle. I also could not lift the heavy pails with gallons of milk. The milk was emptied into the large, aluminum bulk tank where the milk was cooled. My sister worked much harder than I and was much stronger. She milked the cows and lifted the pails of milk above her head to pour the milk into the strainer located on top of the bulk milk tank. One evening, the high-voltage electricity shorted to this huge metal tank. As Elaine began to pour the milk, the electricity traveled up the stream of milk and into Elaine. Never in our lives had we heard such a blood curdling scream. To this day, my heart hurts when thinking of this painful, frightening experience for my sister.

We raised wheat and corn to grind into "grist" for a high protein food. Milk production increases greatly when this is fed to cattle. But besides working to maintain our cattle, Mom also had an acre garden to be planted, hoed and harvested. The garden was in a "kettle hole," left from the last receding glacier in Michigan. It was the most fertile acre on the farm and produced abundantly. We canned hundreds of quarts of everything from green beans and sweetcorn to fruit and tomatoes. Mom canned delicious tomato juice, gallons of it, enough for us for the winter if we rationed it.

In the late evening after milking was done, we swam in Baptist Lake where neighborhood religions baptized their congregations. We popped the popcorn we grew and drank apple cider fresh from the mill.

Mom baked incredible bread and cinnamon rolls and we ate them with home-churned butter. We drank ice cold milk from the bulk milk tank.

Today, milking cattle and raising "feed" is different. I hope it is safer. There are bigger and more automated machines to lift the burden of the farmer, his wife and their children. Farmers now speak in "short speak" and acronyms and talk of agribusiness and GMO's. GPS units direct each perfectly straight tractor trip across the field. Soil type, fertilizer level and water content of the soil are statistics that are automatically fed into computers for analysis. Tractors are air conditioned and "Sting" is never too old to be coming through the ear buds. Still, farming and producing milk is hard work.

New problems and new conversations are arising concerning milk. Milk has a place in politics, the economy, the health of our children, possible shortages and global warming. Perhaps cattle will be replaced with almonds and soybeans, but it is milk that tastes best on cereal. It is a glass of milk that is handed to a child. A good cup of coffee is better with a bit of dairy. All of these thoughts of my childhood have been revisited because of a television commercial. It asked one question, "Got Milk?"

"*Hogs and Kisses*"

Two fat pink pigs were kissing on the white coffee cup that I was "borrowing." It read "hogs and kisses." That is all it took. My mind was instantly gone from my meeting. I had not had time to visit my mom for a little while so nothing was going to stop me from thinking of her now. One of the last chores with my mother involved pigs.

It had been a relatively warm winter day at twenty degrees when I visited Mom at the family farm. The sun was bright and the snow sparkled. I was walking into the farmhouse as my brother, Don, was walking out. Don announced to Mom that he had checked Gertie and she was not going to deliver her piglets until Friday. Don was headed for town to do errands and would be gone for about three hours.

He had just checked his favorite pet, Gertie. She was a white Yorkshire hog, pregnant, and weighed in at about three-hundred and sixty pounds. Don enjoyed scratching Gertie behind the ears as much as Gertie enjoyed being scratched. Don was Gertie's favorite human being. But Gertie was more than a pet to a farmer. She and her litter were a source of income.

Don, like other farmers, must be able to recognize the signs that an animal is soon to give birth to their babies. Farmers assist their animals. Don felt safe to leave Gertie. Don drove his truck past the house, heading to town, Sand Lake, population 164. Within moments, Don's thirteen-year-old son, Dustin, ran into the house and announced, "Grandma, Gertie is having her piglets."

Mom and I dressed for the cold and headed for Gertie. She was in a Quonset hut. The hut was about fifteen feet long, all heavy boiler plate metal, and shaped like a barrel cut in half, lengthwise. We crawled into the small Quonset opening at the end. The hut was filled three-fourths full of straw and litter to keep Gertie warm, which is not too difficult for an animal of Gertie's size. She produced great quantities of body heat.

Our flashlights did not immediately find Gertie. She had dug for herself a deep nest and piled the rest of the bedding high around her.

Mom was able to stand upright on the bedding. At age seventy-eight, she was beginning to shrink. The Quonset accommodated her 4'9" stature beautifully. She stood there in her winter barn clothes including her little burgundy stocking cap. It brushed the one-inch hoar frost that glistened from the ceiling of the icy hut. Our breaths condensed in the cold air.

We had no chance of either digging Gertie out or going into her deep, narrow nest. If we upset her, Gertie could attack, bite, or thrash her heavy weight around. There would never be enough room for the piglets in the hole either. Gertie could lie on each new piglet. Mom would have to rescue each piglet the moment it was born.

Mom lay down on the litter, reached her right arm over the edge of the deep nest, and, trying not to slide over the edge, she caught the first piglet as it was born. For the next three hours, Mom and I were a tag team. She caught each piglet and forward passed each one to me.

I had sent Dustin to the house to get two cardboard boxes to hold the piglets. It would keep them from running out of the Quonset and freezing or falling back down with their mother where she could not keep from lying on them.

It was my job to wipe off each white little piglet and check to see if it was breathing and healthy. I enjoyed my job, and I know Mom did, too. Each Yorkshire piglet was a pinky-white with about a dozen wiry two-inch hairs on its body. As I checked each, their beautiful blue eyes looked back at me. Each looked me in the eye and said, "uuuuuh" as if I had slightly squeezed him. I had not, but pigs do not say "Oink." They do not shape an "O" with their mouths. The sound comes from the back of their throats. It is a soft sound. Oink is harsh. Uuuuh is clearer and softer. It is almost two syllables with the emphasis at the end.

I placed all but one of the piglets in the boxes. I put a light coating of straw on top of them. I listened to the sound of each tiny white toenail tapping the bottom of the boxes. It was constant, like the rain on the steel roof of the farmhouse where my bedroom had been, close to the roof and the rain. The toe-tattoo was mixed with the gentle grunting sounds. Piglets arrive hungry and they are ready to eat. Each arrives with energy and enthusiasm, happily greeting the world.

It took three hours and Gertie was done. We had not lost a piglet but one piglet was not placed in the box. It had been carried by Dustin inside of his coat to the house. There he placed it near the heat from the floor register to gently warm.

Don arrived home. He charged from the truck to the Quonset to his precious Gertie. He saw piglets in boxes and roared, "You did it all wrong!" Mom and I left Don to see to Gertie and her litter. We retreated to the house. Upon entering, the seventeenth piglet raced across the carpet toward us. It hopped, stopped and faced us. Its blue eyes were bright. It was warm and the picture of good health, like its sixteen siblings in the boxes.

Don would go down into Gertie's nest, scratch her behind her ears and talk softly to her. He would expand the area around her, place each piglet on a teat to suckle, and compliment her on such beautiful babies.

We could only feel badly for Don. We had no way of contacting him. We had had the joy of receiving Gertie's piglets into the world. He had been robbed after tending to her so faithfully.

Camp Henry

I helped to work my way through Central Michigan University in Mt. Pleasant by waitressing. I worked at an expensive restaurant called the Steer Haus in Sand Lake along highway 131 North of Grand Rapids. I was so small that I ran around and around the tables delivering food. The professional waitresses, with their long arms, delivered an eight-pound relish tray to each table with ease. Delicacies on the heavy wooden tray included sweet, green figs and spiced apple rings. A huge salad bowl of greens was served with an outstanding blue-cheese house dressing. Then came the steaks. One called the Two-pound Diamond Jim was served on a hot, spattering, sizzle platter. It was dangerous for me, and all of the waitresses, to carry several steaks on one tray. Dessert followed. It was a long meal. I once served to one customer eight Black Russians to drink to finish his meal. It did not help that I had never eaten in a restaurant, did not know the routine, and had never seen an alcoholic drink. I was a horrible waitress. I wanted out.

In the Field House at CMU, I saw a sign hanging on a doorknob asking for someone to teach archery at a church camp for the summer. I was hesitant because I did not know what a camp was, but anything was better than waitressing. I applied and acquired the position.

George and I met at Camp Henry, Westminster Presbyterian Summer Camp, run by Catholics. It just worked out that way because so many prospective teachers at Central were Catholic. The church recruited their camp counselors from CMU.

There were ten counselors and ten more employees to cook and keep us in line. Each counselor kept his own cabin with eight children from the same grade. My girls were fourth graders. A new group arrived each week. Each camp counselor was given a name, not necessarily flattering. George's name was Doc, not bad, but the name I received, I did not think I deserved.

We went through a few days of training and worked at cleaning up the cabins and raking the grounds. On a lunch break, George headed for the pier that jutted into the lake. I saw him fishing, came up behind him and spoke. "Nice fishing rod." He turned and jumped when he saw me. Without hesitation, he handed the rod to me and told me to fish. I did not have any idea of how to fish. In my family, males fished. Females were for cleaning fish. George showed me how to cast and use the rod. I thought that was the kindest thing anyone had ever done for me.

Over the next few days, George taught me how to paddle a canoe and operate a motorboat. Those were joyful days for me as we traveled the local waterway from one small lake to the next.

The head of counseling, Coach, devised a little "comradery competition" for us. He came up with a canoe race. There was to be a guy and a girl in each canoe. The girl was to sit in the stern to paddle and rudder the canoe. The guy was to sit in the bow, facing the girl, not facing the direction the canoe was to be headed. Chuck, one of the counselors, was in the bow. He looked at me with distrust and tried to row backward. He was rocking the canoe, throwing water, and we darted from side to side. I told him to sit still and let me do the work. I took control of the canoe with an even stroke and set our course. We won. George was proud of me.

One of the counselors was huge, muscular, handsome and used to winning. At the end of the race, he was so angry at having lost that he threw his black rimmed glasses tumbling down the beach and he swore. He felt he never should have been placed in a boat with a girl named "Zero."

I had won the race. The only things I could remember having previously won was a cake carrier when I was five years old and a Bazooka Bubble Gum blowing contest when I was eight. Perhaps I had won a boyfriend. I was on a roll.

Black Canyon of the Gunnison National Monument

George was full of surprises. We were not going to live on the North Rim of the Black Canyon, the headquarters side, where people lived. We were to journey to the South Rim, but there is no bridge across the canyon. After checking into headquarters, we drove the ninety miles around to the other side of the canyon. From there, we could see the headquarters we had left behind.

We drove into the rarely visited South Rim of the park and along the one-lane dirt road at the edge of the canyon. The sun was about to set as we approached the Quonset hut. This was to be home for eight weeks. George tried to pick me up and carry me across the threshold, but we struggled with the small, narrow door and tumbled inside. I managed to land on my feet. Tumbling and landing on my feet seemed to be a metaphor for the next forty-three years.

On our first morning, we were awakened by a strange noise, a black steer was scratching his hide on the metal roof of the Quonset. The Quonset was a delightful and secluded place to live. We did not see more than twenty-five visitors the entire summer. The campground was usually empty, but we did haul in a water supply with the water tank. The hot-water heater was old and contaminated with bleach. My hair bleached to a blond for the summer. We had our own wooden outhouse that was clean and smelled good. The wooden bench inside was made to be lifted. That was necessary to check for Black Widow spiders before being seated.

I learned about George that summer. He was easy to live with. He was kind, worked hard, and loved all of nature. But cookies came first. I was trying to do the dutiful wifely things, like bake cookies. I had just removed the cookie sheet from the oven when George grabbed at a hot cookie. I tapped at his knuckles with the spatula and sharped, "You'll get burned." He gave me the most confounded look that I had ever seen on anyone's face. His eyes searched my face, his mouth snapped open in surprise and wordlessly his attitude seemed to say, "You cannot treat me like a child and I will prove it to you." He stole the hot pan of cookies and disappeared. Later that afternoon, I found the empty cookie sheet on the wood pile and baked the rest of the cookie dough.

Everywhere George went, I went. Everything that was broken, we fixed together. We eradicated bull thistles by chopping them out with Pulaski axes. I loved riding with him in the beat-up park pick-up. We never knew what we would see or how late we would return to the Quonset. In the evening, we saw and listened to the coyotes at the small earthen reservoir.

One late evening, the lights from the truck picked up an encounter between an owl and a deer. The large, tan-spotted owl stood in the middle of the dirt road. The doe approached it hesitantly to see what it was. They gently touched, nose to beak, and parted ways, satisfied.

Another time, as we walked a wide graveled path, a golden eagle closed in over our heads and cast his shadow on the ground in front of us. He was waiting for us to scare up a small rodent or a rabbit for him. As he loomed above and behind us, the tiny hairs rose eerily on the backs of our necks as though he were stalking us.

During the day, I would drive to the nearest town of Crawford for groceries. The town was made up of one store that sold everything. Aluminum kettles rose double my height toward the ceiling and the ceiling rose above that. The wooden floor with its narrow slats, concaved ever so gently with each of my footsteps. The deli had one dark, nearly-empty, cooled case containing one tomato and one little beef roast. I asked the price. He said, "Seventy-two cents a pound," embarrassed that it should be so expensive.

While returning from Crawford, I had a flat tire in the desert-land. I was in a hurry to put the groceries from the back seat of the car into the refrigerator. After all, I had dared to buy ice cream that day. It was starting to rain and the temperature was dropping. I changed the tire though I had never changed a tire in my life. I had not hesitated. I had never seen another vehicle on that stretch of dusty road. I could have waited for help for a long time.

Surgery by Flashlight

George and I had been married for five days when he carried me across the threshold into the Quonset hut. We would live there for the summer while working at the Black Canyon of the Gunnison National Monument in Colorado. The monument was a colorful canyon with a great gray and pink wall, side canyons, and brown trout in the Gunnison River, nearly a thousand feet below.

But into the summer, George began to limp. A corrosive grimace marred his handsome face. He was in pain. We discussed the problem and the options. He had had this problem before and it involved surgery, twice. George had an ingrown toenail. I had never heard of such a thing. We envisioned having to drive the twenty miles of narrow dirt road out of the park to the Crawford Dam. There we would pick up the paved road, and drive over an hour to Montrose where we thought there might be a doctor. We could not call as the outpost station did not have a phone.

That evening in bed, I heard him groan. The sheet on us was too much pressure for the sore toe. I told him that I would look at it. We had few medical supplies in the Quonset, not even aspirin as a pain reliever. We had never thought of needing medical help.

He whimpered as he sat on the edge of the bed. Since the power generator had been turned off for the evening, we had no electricity for light. Walking in the dark to the shed to start the generator seemed to be more work than we were willing to do at that late hour. Besides, we had been having trouble with porcupines around the Quonset and one sore toe was bad enough without a foot full of quills.

With the flashlight, I located a bottle of rubbing alcohol and George's Swiss Army knife. I sterilized the knife with the alcohol and the blade with a match. I swabbed the toe with alcohol and I was ready to operate. I gave him the flashlight to point downward to highlight the offending toe. I could see that the big toe of the right foot had an angry spear protruded from under the edge of the toenail. George told me what his previous surgical procedures had been and I said, "I can do that."

I was lying in my pajamas with my belly on the cool painted-concrete floor. My face was over the toe. George angled the flashlight to give me maximum light. The small blade on the bulky Swiss Army knife was sharp. I knew that if I did not do this correctly, it would just grow back again as it had done twice before. It might even become infected. George's summer could be ruined. In the dark, George kept his foot perfectly still and allowed me to do the surgery.

I could see that the sharp spear of nail needed to be removed, but it was caught half-way under the toenail. Each time I moved the spear, I could hear George grind his teeth in pain. I had to hurry because I was hurting him. The base of the spear was healthy flesh but it would have to be cut. I worked the spear into position, cutting it away from under the toenail. I cut the flesh at the base with the knife. I had no tweezers or pliers so I pressed the knife blade under the spear and held my finger tightly on top. I gripped hard and yanked. As George recoiled from the pain, I rolled away on the floor to avoid being kicked in the face.

The next day, the rest of the summer, and the rest of his life, he never had trouble or pain with the toe again. We never did know how far we were from a doctor, nor did we care.

Isle Royale

After I had been with George for two seasons at the Black Canyon of the Gunnison National Monument, he announced that he wanted to work as a boatman on Isle Royale National Park, Lake Superior, Michigan. To be on the water sounded wonderful, so we drove to park headquarters in Houghton-Hancock on the Keewenaw Peninsula in the Upper Peninsula. We boarded the baby-blue Ranger III on the "big waters" to the islands. We would soon find that Lake Superior is appropriately named. Its beauty and danger are superior to all other bodies of water.

Classes were held at the beginning of the summer season for new and returning rangers. We stayed at Rock Harbor, the island headquarters, while George and I attended the orientation classes. In the morning, George was handed the keys to the Demoray, a twenty-five-foot garbage scow with a three-quarter inch boiler plate hull. With the keys, George became an official National Park Service Boat Patrol Ranger.

We put all of our provisions for the summer, from winter clothing to towels and bedding, into the Demoray. We were also given a full-sized refrigerator to take to the cabin. It was lashed on the starboard side in the stern. Again, I was to be the first woman to occupy this outpost station, the cabin at Malone Bay on the southern edge of the island. Therefore, a refrigerator was important for a woman to have to maintain a home.

We were excited. George was piloting his first park service boat. We traveled the length of Rock Harbor that is protected on both sides by walls of rock. The brilliant sun reflected off the white tops of the blue waves. At the exit into the main lake, we cut south and then south-west toward Malone Bay. We immediately picked up fog, wind and large waves. This is an unusual combination, and this was not a good time or place for George to learn how to drive a boat or navigate Lake Superior.

The waves grew higher and the fog settled a few feet above the boat. The extra weight, George and the refrigerator on the starboard side, tipped the bow off course. We could not quarter the waves to head north toward the south side of the island. The compass was useless. It did not swing back and forth in a general direction but flipped and twirled like a pinwheel. We were lost. Also, with each wave, the refrigerator started to eject out of the boat. I stiff-armed it against each wave to keep it in the boat. Wrong thing to do! I should have deep-sixed it. That would have righted the boat.

We had been on our own for one hour when we radioed Rock Harbor for help. Joe, whom we would meet and thank later, was in the small plane, a Cessna, that helped to service the island. He started to look for us but could not find us in the fog. I told George that I heard the plane far to the right of us. We had traveled nearly due south. When Joe finally found us, he said, "You are so far off course that you are headed for Wisconsin. Head north now or you will be outside the small, barrier islands and will not be able to return to the main island."

Turning around any boat in heavy seas is frightening. Waves are said to come in sevens with the seventh wave being the biggest. The pilot must study and count the waves. That seventh wave must be allowed to pass under the boat. At the top of the next wave, the boat must be pivoted, turned around, and allowed to slide down the crest of the wave. This is to keep from being buried in water, broadsided or tipped over. I did not know if the boat would respond quickly enough to turn around, or if the propellers would ride high and burst out of the water. If that happened, the boat would lose traction with the water and we would be either pushed over or dropped like a rock to the bottom of the trough, out of control.

George caught the wave perfectly. We seemed to sit at the top of the wave forever. I was riding far above the trough of the wave. Like a bronco rider on high, I was unable to see the water, only the blue-tinged fog on all sides. We slid down the wave crest and did not crash at the bottom. We did not ram the wave straight on and bury the bow under water. George was able to quarter it at a safe angle. We headed north-east past the barrier islands where the wind and waves subsided.

We reached Malone Bay after a harrowing trip. George was exhausted from having fought every wave. I do not remember much conversation as we trudged up the steep path to the cabin. We carried a few provisions up the hill. This was the first minute I saw the sturdy wooden cabin that would be our home for eight weeks.

I scraped the bachelor-bacon grease off the stove with a screw driver and heated something to eat. Then I set up our home.

George had always said he would rather be lucky than good. That day, he was good, and we were lucky. Joe had located us and given directions to safety. We had come close to taking a drink of the brink on our first experience with Lake Superior, beautiful and dangerous. A more sane wife would have insisted, never again.

Strawberries with Moose

Since early June, George and I had lived at the Malone Bay Ranger Station on Isle Royale National Park in Lake Superior. It was late July and the wild strawberries were ripe. I knew where there was a patch with a fifteen-foot radius. Considering the rough terrain, trees, lack of soil and the fact that Isle Royale is cold on the 48th parallel, that was a good-sized patch.

The patch was only one-third of a mile from the cabin. The trail led to Siskiwit Lake, the largest lake on the largest island in the largest lake in North America. The strawberries were just off the trail in a small clearing not far from the lake.

I was down on all fours picking strawberries. They are tiny and grow very close to the ground. My knees and blue jeans were wet and stained red from squashed berries. My hands were sticky and smelled like jam.

I picked until I heard a rustle to my left. I stopped to check it out, but I saw nothing. I resumed picking. A few minutes later, I heard a "snort." Not a high-pitched, dry tone, but a blow, an exhale that is moist. I thought, "Animals say snort."

I glanced to the left where I had originally heard the rustle. Nothing was there. But, in a heartbeat, I looked up, face forward. A female moose was sniffing the top of my head. She was trying to figure out what type of animal I was, crawling on the ground. I was eye-to-eye with her and still down on all fours when I saw her ears go backward and tighten against her head.

When the ears go back on a cow moose, it means she is about to kick the life out of you. There are better ways to die. I knew when to run! I had no idea what happened to the berries I had picked, nor did I care. I did not stop running and I did not look back until I reached the cabin.

Aurora Borialis

The park service boat was a garbage scow with a three-eighths inch boiler-plate hull. We collected the garbage from the few campsites on the southern shore and hauled cargo to and from Mott Island Headquarters. The heavy hull gave protection from sharp rocks and reefs. The rocky islands were volcanic snags grasping to bring down ships. The rocks were amygdaloidal basalt, with empty holes or holes filled with shiny green stones called chlorastrolite. This is the second gemstone of Michigan.

The weather was reported to the park each morning from the MAFOR. It stands for Marine Forecast and is broadcast over the radio. It was given in number code. One number in each line was to be circled with pencil and deciphered. Since the islands are in Lake Superior, weather was often dangerous. In one week, we had three gales with forty-five knot winds. The waves crashed on rock crags. The fog was called pea soup. Worse days were called peasoupers. But, when the storms would break, the islands with their rocky shores were splashed in brilliant white waves. The rays of sun light would shine through the noisy spray.

It was either the danger of the rocks or the bounty of the island. The great storms were followed by brilliant sunshine. It was always that way, always the extremes of Isle Royale.

One stormy evening, George and I retired to our bed in the ranger cabin. We were exhausted from working in the cold, foul weather. The heavy rain beating on the metal roof was so noisy that we had little conversation. It hammered us to sleep. At three a.m. we were awakened by bright light and the sound of silence. We did not understand the source of the light or the silence. We dressed in heavy coats and exited the cabin. We took the slippery trail through the wet trees to the dock. From there we looked skyward. The aurora borealis filled the sky with long green and pink flowing curtains. Back and forth they waved. We stood, watching in awe, mouths open and heads held back. Our neck muscles began to burn so we lay on the cold, wet, wooden dock and stared upward. We refused to retreat to the cabin until the decorator colors faded in the dawn.

"Gilligaloobirds"

Isle Royale is an ecological wonder. The layers of the earth have tipped on their sides almost ninety degrees creating wave after wave of ridges. The ridges are high and dry while the troughs between are filled with brush, pine trees, swamps and small lakes. The wolf vs. moose relationship has been studied there since the early 1970s. Fishermen families still make their living there within the park. There are lighthouses and sunken ships. It has sour thimbleberries and thumb-nail size blueberries. It has chlorastrolite, better known as greenstone, and a rugged layered geology. Siskiwit Lake on the island, has the original lamprey-free Lake trout. The park is an archipelago with hundreds of islands, sharp rocks, that rise out of the water to grab sailors like Scylla and Charybdis.

George was called The Malone Bay Ranger! Yes, it reminds you of the *William Tell Overture*. No, you do not have to say, "Hi, oh, Silver, away!" We were the only occupants of the Malone Bay Ranger Station until the very end of our second summer. A friend, a school principal, needed to report for work earlier than we teachers. He asked if his son Mike could finish out the summer with us. Certainly he could. No problem. He was a great middle-school kid who cut up his own salad to keep the carrots from breaking his braces.

During the summer, George had piloted the Demoray, a twenty-four-foot heavy-duty work boat. But the engine had quit. A twenty-two-foot open aluminum fishing boat was its replacement for us. We went from a 280 horse-power inboard to a 45 horse-power outboard motor to navigate the waves of Lake Superior. It was not a good substitution.

When it was time for us to return home to our classrooms, three people and nine-weeks of summer belongings would not fit in the aluminum boat. We had nineteen miles of open water to travel to park headquarters at Rock Harbor. From there, the beautiful, baby-blue Ranger III would transport us across Lake Superior. We would unload in Houghton/Hancock on the Keweenaw Peninsula, the mainland of Michigan.

Since we could not make the trip in an unsafe open boat to Rock Harbor, a dare-devil ranger was coming to get us. He was tall, lean, and handsome with a devil-may-care attitude. His salt and pepper dark hair was Errol Flynn wavy. He had the mustache that went with the whole affect. He looked great in a National Park Service uniform.

When I heard he was coming for us, I had second thoughts. The open aluminum boat was looking better. This man was bringing a twenty-eight-foot pleasure craft piloted from inside the cabin. It looked like a tight-butted Spanish galleon. It was top heavy and needed a ton of rocks and concrete in the hold to keep the top of the boat from waving in the breeze like its own flag.

The term "gilligaloobirds" came to mind. It was coined by an older, lovable man who worked on the island. We called him "IBM," Italian Boat Mechanic. Since he was the one who fixed the broken boats, his term, "gilligaloobirds," meant bobbing about like a bird on the waves. The one coming for us was without a care, reckless and dangerous.

I had ridden with him once before. The boat had stunk badly of gasoline. That unnerved me. Someone must have complained because, after my trip with him, a maintenance crewman pumped gallons of gasoline and water out of the bilge. He had come close to blowing us up. He did not take care of equipment or details. He seemed to be in the park service for the fun, the out-of-doors, and the toys that come with a higher position. He was rough and tumble. He bragged that his favorite meal was steak and popcorn. One tough constitution!

He arrived in his galleon at Malone Bay on a rough, wet and gray day. It was the end of the summer and Lake Superior was giving up its heat. That accounted for the thick fog that made us wonder if there was air to be breathed. The waves would be high. Without smiles, we loaded the boat. George and I did not feel good about the situation, especially having twelve-year old Mike with us. People stop smiling when they are responsible for a friend's child. I had little faith in our transportation. In contrast, it was always safety first with George.

There are buoy markers all around the islands to mark safe passage. Two black and white painted barrels marked the passageway into and out of Malone Bay. From the cabin, one safely travels slightly southwest, between the barrels, continues traveling for five minutes and then cuts northeast, a straight shot to Rock Harbor. If you follow the markers, you avoid all reefs.

We began our trip. Our pilot opened the throttle. One usually adjusts the speed to the condition of the waves, but he did not. We "gilligaloobirded" it. He did not bother with the barrels. He cut southeast. The chart showed several reefs, but the lake was high that summer and we skinned over them.

I had never been that close to the giant southern rock point in my life. My stomach dropped and I looked at George. He looked scared and rarely had I seen that countenance. He quietly told me that he would stand outside of the cabin, on the small stern deck, and watch for reefs. Mike joined him. I sat inside the cabin by the window and stared through the fog at the outline of the main island.

We were a long way from Rock Harbor when I screamed, "Schooner Island's too close!" From the stern came, "Reef!" Our pilot yanked both throttles toward himself, killing the engine. We hit the reef, dead on, but we were going so fast, with so much power, that our propeller wave, our "prop wash," picked us up, banged us down on top of the reef and proceeded to grind the bottom of the boat across the reef. Grind right, grind left, grind right and the prop wash deposited us on the opposite side of the wide reef.

Immediately, I raised the floorboards to see if we had punctured the bottom of the boat and were possibly taking on water. We were not. Had we destroyed the shaft or propeller? No, the boiler-plate bottom had taken the brunt of the force. Shaft and propeller had never hit the reef.

The prop wash from our own foolish, high speed had saved us. We had been saved by serendipitous stupidity.

Had we lost the propeller or bent the shaft, we would have made a May Day call. But, no one could have saved us. The waves would have crashed us against the high rock walls of the island. We could not have survived the cold water.

Our pilot started the engine and then chirped, "No harm, no foul!" He pushed both throttles forward, full bore, and we were off again like gilligaloobirds.

Lansing Fire Ball

We headed home to Dearborn from Isle Royale National Park on a gorgeous day aboard the Ranger III. It was a great trip on Lake Superior to the Michigan mainland. We found our vehicle that had been parked for the summer in Houghton near park headquarters. We were returning to teach in our class rooms in two days, the day after Labor Day.

But there was a problem. No matter how slowly George drove, I kept telling him to slow down. Fifty miles per hour was scary. We had not traveled that fast all summer since our only travel had been by boat. It was white-knuckle driving until we were forced to catch up to the speed of traffic. Eventually, we calmed down and enjoyed mainland Michigan's solid ground. It is not unusual to feel a sense of acceleration on land if you have been on water for a long period of time.

We got as far south as Lansing when the weather turned on us. The sky became gray, ugly, and dangerous. Rain dropped so hard on us that the wind shield wipers could not keep the window clear. Visibility dropped to a few feet. Drivers slowed their speed and then slowed again. We closely followed the tail lights of the vehicle ahead of us.

What happened next is best described as a brilliant ball of lightning that exploded in the sky. It was not a bolt; it was a perfectly round yellow explosion. It was nothing like I had ever seen. It was followed by a crack of thunder so intense that we felt it shove its pressure down on us and reverberate off the highway. I screamed one loud and painful scream. Though it seemed impossible, the rain increased. Drivers followed by inches in back of the vehicle in front of them. If they did not drive closely, they would lose sight of the slight red glow of the brake lights in front of them and be lost.

I have heard of Texas rains where one cannot stand outside for fear of drowning. This was it. Water, an inch deep, was on the skin of the car. We were submerged by the rain. The next few minutes seemed to take forever. As slowly as we were driving, we could not have traveled more than a few miles.

By the time the rain subsided, we were exhausted. My chest felt crushed and our bodies were vibrating inside and out. George had an empty stare and did not release his grip on the wheel. We had never heard of an exploding ball of lightning like the phenomenon we had experienced.

Margo ... Margo ... Margo ...

Margo hit the park like a small atom bomb. She arrived from California where she was president of COYOTE, the prostitution union she had formed. COYOTE stands for Cast Off Your Old Tired Ethics. This was quite scathing for 1974. Each day, George would come in from work and tell me a new Margo story. Margo had greeted her reason for being in the park by charging him, throwing her long, un-shaven legs and hiking boots around his waist. The kiss was quite remarkable. Her short shorts were blue jean cut-offs, the new style frowned-upon by society. I was told when Margo did things in the park like hike the trails topless. I knew when she hiked to the fire lookout to spend a few days with her friend. George verbalized that he wondered how she could be a prostitute when she was so homely. George was fascinated with her and the stories he heard about her.

Margo ... Margo ... Margo ...

George was the patrol ranger on Ross Lake in the North Cascades National Park where Margo was visiting. The Cascade Mountains, the "Alps" of the Great Northwest, are young in comparison to the Rocky or Appalachian Mountains. Hiking trails are sharp dynamite-blasted granite. The newest thing in sports equipment "back then" was thick Vibram soles on new Vasque mountain-hiking boots. Avid hikers could wear the Vibram through on the jagged rocks by the end of the summer.

Rimmed by those beautiful mountains, Ross Lake is an eighteen-mile long lake in a deep canyon. It is south to north with the last half mile across the border into Canada. At the southern end, Ross Lake Dam added to the height of the lake, making it a reservoir. The dam created the electricity for Seattle City Light Power. The lake was deep, dark and dangerous. As the water rose, it created new, narrow side canyons. Maidenhair ferns grew in the cracks on the steep walls.

Lightning Creek flowed into Lightning Creek Canyon, so narrow that, even at high noon, sunlight did not hit the water below. Into its dark shadows, rainbow trout had been stocked by researchers. They were not minnow size, but large juveniles. Each trout had been brightly tagged through the base of the dorsal fin. They were perfectly shaped, beautifully colored, healthy and off limits to fishermen.

It was George's job to protect the natural resources. That included checking Lightning Creek to keep fishermen from taking the tagged rainbow trout. George entered the canyon, followed the walls to where his Boston whaler ran out of space on both sides, and discovered a poacher.

The poacher was about sixty, overweight, and grayingly grizzled. He was mild mannered and, obviously, neither violent nor wealthy. But, he had caught and killed thirty-two of the planted fish. They lay in the bottom of the old boat, their beauty destroyed. George, disgusted, considered arresting the man and taking his boat and fishing equipment. But, that would be mean to someone who could not afford to lose so much. It would also be more trouble than it was worth.

How would George get the poacher and his boat and equipment out of the canyon, off the lake, and up the one-mile hiking trail to the road? There he would have to wait for a patrol car. From there, the poacher would be driven the many miles to the nearest jail cell. It would be enough trouble to confiscate all of the fish and get them into a freezer to save as evidence. But George had to do more than just give him a ticket. Therefore, he issued a ticket with a mandatory court appearance.

The man would have to take a day off of work and drive to the courthouse. He would lose a day's pay, have a court record and pay a large fine. George, being the ranger who had written the ticket as a mandatory court appearance, had to report to court to testify against him.

George arrived in court to discover a new, young judge who knew nothing about fish, fishing, or fishing regulations. It was obvious that he would never be able to figure out why fishermen never put their fishing reel anywhere they would not place their sandwich.

The poacher pled not guilty.

George took the stand and the judge asked George how he knew the man was guilty of poaching. George relayed the circumstances of the narrow canyon and the dead fish. He then asked George, "What is the usual fine for poaching?" George answered, "Ten dollars, your honor." The judge then said, "I fine the gentleman ten dollars." George had meant, "Ten dollars per fish." Too late! George's eyes flew open and his jaw dropped. The poacher did everything he could to keep from laughing aloud. He ducked his head and hid his face to keep from chortling. George was in shock! The judge then asked George, "What do you plan to do with the fish?" George answered emphatically, "I plan to biologically destroy them!" George was going to get something out of this. He would savor every bite! He would eat them all!

Later that summer, we were invited to a Thanksgiving Day picnic. Summers in North Cascades National Park are so short that Christmas and Thanksgiving can be celebrated at any time and in any order. When we arrived for the feast, George was grabbed by the happy hostess and escorted to the head of the lineup of picnic tables. I was placed at the end table where I sat with a young woman who was breast-feeding her baby. I could see that George was going to have more fun than I. George had been placed across from Margo ... Margo ... Margo. Margo spoke familiarly to George, which surprised him as he had never met her. George turned pink. Obviously, she had been told of George's fish-poaching and court story because she smiled with a coy little look and said, "Hello, George. I understand that you and I have a lot in common. We both have trouble with judges."

But There was Once ...

George and I lived on a two-hundred-foot raft called the "float." It served as the Ross Lake Ranger Station in the North Cascades National Park. Our house on the float had two rooms. It had no water so we had no shower or sanitary facilities. Our source of heat was my oven. The three of us lived there, George, ten-week old Matthew, and I. George did the boat patrols and I took care of the daily family needs. This was the third outpost station where I was the first woman to live.

I greeted all of the people who came through. I met the trail crew, the Sherpa groups, visitors, fishermen and the brass. Daily chores included dipping a twenty-gallon coffee pot overboard to boil water to cool for the next day's drinking supply. I cooked, baked, carried Matt and the dirty laundry up the mile-long trail to the top of the canyon to take to Concrete, WA. There, I did the banking, laundry, and grocery shopping. I also did all the small jobs requested of me.

Female, small, quiet, obedient, afraid of everything, I learned early that I was to be unseen and unheard. My father knew that when I opened my mouth, I would stick my foot into it, royally. He thought I would tell secrets and embarrass my family. For the majority of my life, I have kept my mouth shut.

But there was once ...

There are injustices in this world to be protested. It was a quiet day on the reservoir and George was out on boat patrol. It was cold and the air was a light gray fog. District Ranger Tim showed up unannounced.

My cabin was warm and spotless. Baby Matthew was asleep and I sat with my usual afternoon snack, peanuts and a tankard of hot tea.

Tim was a good district ranger. He looked to details. This is always the sign of a good ranger. He stood the straightest of any ranger I had ever seen. His uniform was perfect, his flat hat sat on his head at the exact angle of 180 degrees. No wind could possibly have dislodged it. He did not remove the hat during our pleasant conversation. He sat ramrod straight when he announced his plan to arrange a treat for all of the rangers. He was going to book a flight in a small plane around Mt. Baker for each of his men. It was a geologist's dream and a ranger's reward for jobs well done.

That year, Mt. Baker, a gorgeous Washington state volcano, had become active. The snow was black at the top of the mountain from the fumes and volcanic ash. The vent at the top had become so gaping that blocks of glacial ice the size of football fields dropped into the maw. Geologists and volcanologists were worried. Where was the water disappearing? Would Mt. Baker become more active? Would it erupt?

Then, I opened my mouth. I told him of the unfairness of this. He was treating the men well. I blurted, "Well, what about me?" In one big gush I said, " I was the one who drove the truck up the face of the dam when there were no men around." At no other time would I have been allowed to touch the truck, except when they needed help.

"I drove the boat across the lake when a trail crew was dropped off and there were no men to pilot the boat back." At no other time was I allowed to touch the boats.

And, a well-run ranger station was proof of my worth.

The poor sweet man. I had blasted him. I did not think he could sit any straighter, but he managed. He was in shock. His eyes were round and unblinking through his wire rimmed glasses. His eyes, the glass and the rims sparkled, and I was looking right at those blue eyes. This was a challenge.

I am not sure what happened next. Did he say it was time to leave? Was George going to lose his job? Would George never forgive my big mouth? I suffered.

Several days later, we drove to the float plane landing. George and other rangers disappeared down the gravel ramp to a small storage and warming hut. I could not see the men or the plane. I stayed at the car with Matthew who was asleep in the back seat.

I could just hear my name being called by my friend Donna. She was the wife of one of the naturalists who was on the plane. She was running and slipping up the loose-graveled ramp when she said, "Judy, they are waiting at the plane for you." She insisted that I go and she volunteered to stay with Matthew. I sprinted for the plane and we flew.

The North Cascade Mountains were covered with more snow than I had ever seen in one place. Below me, on Mt. Baker, actual glaciers were under assault by volcanic heat. There were acres of black ash. And I was sitting in a four-seater, single engine airplane, so noisy that no one bothered to utter a word. We just peeked out of the small dirty windows in awe.

I never saw Tim again to thank him, but his kindness serves as a reminder that, once, I opened my mouth.

A Tribute to Bertram Boats

It was our second year on Ross Guard Station on Ross Lake Reservoir in North Cascades National Park, Washington. George was the boat patrol ranger on Ross Lake. That summer, we had brought ten-week old, baby Matthew. We took him everywhere with us. He did not fuss when we explored steep mountain roads. We made descents that were so steep that the transmission and the brakes smoked. The fuel lines dripped onto the hot manifold and they smoked as well. Most of the time, Matthew was in a short, canvas crib in the back of the Jeep or he was in the Jerry Pack on my back. He slept soundly in the boat whenever we traveled on the lake. It was a wonderful experience to keep our baby close at all times.

Stew and Donna Fritts were friends who worked at the park with us. Stew was a naturalist with an incredible sense of humor. His off-duty t-shirt showed a warn hiking boot stepping on snapped ferns and the words, "Fern Stomper." Donna worked forest service that summer. She was Italian, and George loved her cooking. I loved their laughter. It was a treat when they visited the guard station. We did strange things like set a fancy, pretentious dinner on the guard station deck and pretend Andy Warhol wanted to paint us with the mountains in the background.

A Ross Lake meeting was to be held eighteen miles "up lake" where the U.S. meets the International Border of Canada. Stew and Donna joined us at the end of the work day for a late afternoon boat ride to the border campground at Hozomeen. If Stew and Donna were to drive a car to the meeting, they would have had to leave six hours early, drive north to enter Canada, and head east to the campground. They would not have been able to attend.

We, the five of us, situated ourselves into the covered twenty-foot Bertram boat. The lake was as flat as a giant piece of black glass. There were no ripples on the water as we headed north. At the equator, the sun sets in the west. The farther north one is, the sun does not set true west, but farther north. It was a blinding sunset that reflected off the flat water as we headed north.

Since we had more weight in the boat, it was necessary to get the boat up on plane to keep from plowing water at the bow. If a boat is on plane, the trip is faster, more comfortable, and less gasoline is use. Riding in the Bertram was my favorite thing to do and I was excited to be included in the trip. Bertrams are powerful and have sleek lines. It gave us a fast, smooth ride.

We traveled half way, as far as the slight dog-leg to the west, when we hit something. The boat stopped dead in the water. George checked the inboard/outboard engine to find half of it dangling from its "umbilical cords." The transmission lines hung deep in the water. Floating a foot deep in the water and undetectable while traveling, we saw the submerged log we had hit. Before logs become totally "waterlogged" and drop to the bottom of the lake, they float just below the surface of the water, then maybe a foot down, then a little more and finally they turn one end down and dive to the bottom. This was the log we had hit with the propeller. It looked as though we had chopped it with an axe.

We did not know if we had done any damage to the bottom of the boat, but I have a reason for loving a twenty-foot Bertram. The boat is next to impossible to sink. The open cab roof is stuffed with flotation where most boats have none, not even bigger Bertrams. There was little reason to panic, but we did have baby Matthew to think about. If the boat had filled with water, I would have been sitting on the roof holding my baby. I would have battled anyone for the position.

Our distress call, "Mayday, mayday, mayday," was answered immediately from three directions. John Anderson, the young and capable ranger who shared the work with George on the southern half of the lake, arrived in under five minutes. Hozomeen and headquarters in Diablo, both answered our call. We were evacuated from the Bertram to a Boston Whaler that had been piloted down lake from Hozomeen. We continued north.

It was still impossible to tell if we had put a hole in the bottom of the boat. Therefore, the boat had to be pulled from the water as quickly as possible. If the boat became waterlogged, it would be too heavy to pull to shore. It would sink to the roof and be blown eventually to anyplace on the lake. There, it would smash to pieces on the rocks. The Bertram was towed back to the guard station by John in the small Boston Whaler where he shoved it onto the gravel launch area.

I do not remember if the business conducted that evening in Hozomeen was important or not, but I do remember sleeping in a bunk bed in a cabin with others in their bunks. Matthew slept safely on the floor beside me in a bureau drawer. The next day, we were ushered home, back to the guard station, minus the Bertram.

That morning, the district rangers from headquarters visited the guard station. The Bertram was winched onto its trailer. George was as surprised as all of us to see the damage that had been done. The boat had split, nearly stem to stern, with two eleven-foot cracks along the lower chines of the boat. Each crack had opened to three inches wide. George knew his life-long dream of being a National Park Service Ranger for years to come was in jeopardy

The interrogation would begin. The questions were expected. Where were you going? Was this official business? Why were you traveling in the evening? Why were you traveling so fast? Why did you have others in the boat? Why could you not see the obstruction?

George was always aware of his surroundings and the safety of every situation. These were easy questions for him to answers, but it is difficult to allow oneself to be judged by those who have never piloted a boat.

It is also difficult to be judged by those who do not understand your work and cannot do your job. But Jerry Woods was George's immediate boss. He was the fairest man on the planet, a great ranger and a great boss. He knew boating, the lake, sunken logs and the dangers of it all. He knew George had responded admirably when we were in danger.

Jerry recognized a good ranger when he saw one and spoke in George's favor. George went on to serve as a National Park Service ranger for another thirty-six seasons.

Later, Jerry brought a gift for Matthew to the guard station in a wadded piece of newspaper. It was a revolving music box with a charming, ceramic little boy.

To My Beloved Matthew 3-4-5

3. opertopiter he said
4. helicopter was my correction
5. His word sang prettier than mine.

3. four years old
4. He is teaching me
5. to hear through new ears.

3. "mist"appeared he said
4. disappeared was my correction
5. His word was more descriptive than mine.

3. four years old
4. He is teaching me
5. to see through new eyes.

Annie

I could tell that Annie was going to be a tough daughter before she was born. At eight months of pregnancy, I would tickle my abdomen to play with her. There was no play. She kicked the heck out of me and beat me with her unborn fists. The number of things that she was destined to do to test my patience was infinite.

When she was three, I saw fine, horizontal cuts around her little fingers. I could not figure out what was happening to create these cuts. One evening, I heard the battery powered pencil sharpener whirring in the den. I bolted to her. There she stood, all twenty-eight inches of her, with her finger in the sharpener. She had found it stashed away in a drawer in the big oak desk. She was fascinated that, if she stuck her finger into the hole, it made a whirring sound. Keeping Annie safe was a chore.

On another occasion, as we traveled West, the temperature was in the nineties and the brilliant sky was colorless. We stopped early at a motel that advertised a large, outdoor, covered pool. We put on bathing suits and headed out of our room. Annie could not swim yet at the age of three, but she was fast, always running ahead of me. As she ran, I yelled for her to stop. Being the child she was, she picked up speed and launched herself into the deep end of the pool.

I dove into the pool and fished her out. I pushed her onto the pool's edge, but she jumped back in at a deeper place. I fished her out again. I held onto the edge of the pool with one hand and shoved her over the lip of the pool. This was difficult for me. I had to dive to bring her up, I could not touch the bottom of the pool to stand, and I am a poor swimmer. She was having such a good time that I decided to let her have her fun. She delighted in the danger. I fished her out no fewer than eighteen times. She seemed to be playing "no mercy for Mommy." I was exhausted.

Later that evening, after baths and dinner, I put her and Matt to bed. I was so ready for sleep. We had put the light out but then we heard a racket coming from Anne's bed. When we put on the lights, we found her with her eyes closed and dog paddling up the side of the bed's headboard. She was reliving her swimming experience. I grabbed her and put her back into bed. Once again, I fell asleep, and once again, Anne woke us up with a racket. She was dog paddling, climbing up the head board. Her eyes were closed and her face was raised. She was holding her breath to reach the top of the water. As I re-tucked her into bed, I wondered if she would let us sleep.

At two a.m., she woke us again while swimming up the edge of the head board, eyes closed, and mouth puckered to take a first breath out of the water. This time I ordered, "Annie, get out of the pool and stay out!" She slept the rest of the night. Later, I chuckled. This difficult little precious blond had done as she had been commanded. Neat! A victory for Mom.

Totality

My Annie flew into Portland, Oregon, from Bellingham, Washington at the same time I flew in from Dearborn, Michigan. We headed for the Pacific coast in a rental car to a three-room cottage surrounded by tall, large-head, white daisies. Our view was of the Oregon coast and the Pacific Ocean. The cottage was situated on a high bluff, and so the fun began.

We watched our step as we descended the semi-washed out path on the edge of the bluff to the beach below. The vertical course was a combination of concrete steps, wooden steps, broken concrete, a horizontal aluminum ladder on a board, and a short jump onto the wet sand at the bottom. For the increase in price for the weekend of the Total Solar Eclipse, I may have been expecting an elevator.

The ocean was at low tide and the beach was expansive. We checked tidal pools and found things we had never seen before. This was followed by a whale watch from Newport, the smallest harbor in the world. We boarded a thirty-foot fishing boat with a young pilot and exited the harbor. We passed under a green bridge with cars passing two hundred feet above our heads. Whales were spotted immediately and we saw them continuously for an hour, until our rental time was over. Later, we ate at the Ocean Restaurant, recommended to us by the local population. It was terrific. I recommend the tuna steak salad.

It was a wonderful five days, but this was not all we were here to see. The date was August 21, 2017, the day of the Total Solar Eclipse,

Totality. We had chosen our spot on the beach to watch the eclipse, but the morning of the 21st was thick with fog. Should we stay or should we leave the beach house and drive inland to watch the sky event? We checked the local weather and it said it would clear. A half an hour later, it said it was not going to clear for several hours. We loaded everything of ours into the rental car and drove north. We stopped at the first town, Newport, for gasoline.

In Oregon, it is a law that an attendant must pump the gas for the customer. A fine-looking young man pumped the gas. He was obviously a local. He said, if he had a chance to leave the gas station, he would forget about driving north to a main highway. It was predicted to be gridlocked with the cars of the million people who had descended upon this area for the eclipse. He would get on the local highway out of town, drive five miles, and go up the "big hill" and stop. The hill top would be in the sunshine and it would be a great place to watch the eclipse.

We took his advice, but upon driving up the big hill, the fog had not dissipated. We drove twenty miles inland and stopped at an intersection where there were no trees or fog, just brilliant sunshine. A few cars had already parked off the road. Folks were setting out their woven chairs, lowering tail gates on pick-up trucks to sit on, and putting sun screen on their children. They put hats on their babies and spread blankets in the small newly mowed meadow. We saw the farmer and his house, equipment and sheds near-by. He was outside and willing to share his meadow for so important an event. No one talked loudly. The intersection was quiet like the moments before a great orchestral concert. The road did not have any traffic or noise. It was time for everyone to put on their eclipse glasses.

Anne and I were in the middle of the small meadow. It was glasses time. We watched the first tiny occlusion of the sun. We knew it would take an hour before totality. We chatted, laughed, and took "selfies." When the sun was about one-third occluded, a breeze started to flow over us. The temperature was cooling and our skin responded with tiny goosebumps.

The first 30 minutes seemed to go by rapidly. The ground took on a golden-green hue. The sun looked like a half moon; it progressed to look like a banana. A small, noisy flock of little birds, close to the ground, flew up and down in a bobbing motion. They seemed confused and unable to make up their minds how to fly together as a flock.

Soon, all that was left of the sun was the Cheshire Cat's grin. Totality was so near that onlookers did a count down from ten. It was three, two, one and the sun blinked out. We cheered, whooped and applauded and, as one, we tore off our glasses. Everyone rose as if in encore. It was safe for us to look at the sun for the fastest two minutes and thirty-eight seconds of our lives. We gaped and grinned. It was a brown sun. Giant gray rays radiated for millions of miles into space. The tiniest corona was visible, complete with Bailey's beads, the changes in elevation on the moon. And there was Venus, showing brilliantly in the sky at 10:08 in the morning.

People were happy and noisy. Exploded anticipation. We watched until a sudden ray of light burst from the upper, far right of the sun. As one, our small crowd recoiled and exclaimed, "Ohhhhhh, right in my eye!" How could we have been so surprised at a burst of ray when we were looking at the sun? We replaced our glasses on our eyes and watched a reverse eclipse performance.

While many people left, Anne and I stayed for the entire three hours to watch the total uncovering of the sun. It seemed to uncover slowly, so we picked the juicy blackberries that grow everywhere on the west side of Oregon. They are hard to keep trimmed back and are a delicious nuisance.

All main arteries to the Portland airport were clogged for hours, so we took a different route. GPS's are great. We were never in the gridlock of thousands of cars on the main highway heading for the Portland airport. We stopped to visit friends in Silverton, close to Portland. The next day, Tom, our friend, Anne and I hiked in large Sitka spruce trees in an area with ten waterfalls. We played with their adorable young dog. The next day, we drove to the airport where Anne and I ate fresh supper salads. We held each other and said few words. We had already said so many. We proceeded to our gates at opposite ends of the airport. Annie said, "I'll see you at Christmas."

The Otter Family

The otter family lived in the bank among the exposed pine tree roots. They lived in the cool shadows at the far side of the marina. Few people knew they were there, but ten-year old Matthew knew. He had seen them with his father. His father drove the big boat with the blue light on top. It was used to keep people safe on the Big Lake.

It was one of those quiet nights at Bridge Bay Marina. No boats were coming in late. There were no wind-ripples on the water. But Matt's sharp eyes saw something in the water coming his direction. It was the otter family. There were five. The two larger ones were the father and mother. They led the way and the three small ones followed. They were two sisters and a slightly smaller brother.

The first to exit the water and land on the dock was the father. As with all otter, he immediately started to mark his territory. He began peein' and ah poohin' on the dock as he walked. Mother otter slipped out of the water and began peein' and ah poohin' and followed her mate. In turn, the three siblings slipped out of the water and onto the deck. Each began peein' and ah poohin' as was expected of them.

For a short time, the adults investigated man-made objects. They sniffed the ropes that securely tied the boats to the docking cleats. They sniffed the bait buckets, the metal stairs and boat motors. They found nothing of interest. There were no fish to eat. Otters are always on the lookout for food. It was time to search someplace else.

Father and mother slipped into the water first and began swimming into dark-shadows. The two sisters followed their parents. They were looking ahead and not backward. They did not notice that junior did not follow them into the water. He had wandered off in search of his own adventure. Suddenly, he realized that he was alone.

He scurried to the edge of the wooden walkway but did not plunge into the dark water. He cried, "Yip! ... Yip! ... Yip!" This was otter talk for, "Don't leave me behind!" His sisters turned at the sounds of his distress. They swam back toward their brother. They, too, cried "Yip! ... Yip! ... Yip!" He stood at the edge of the walk on three little feet. His sleek, dark body made anxious jerking motions as he peered for his sisters. The sisters yipped again to entice him into the water. He followed their call, slipped off the walkway and into the water. The sisters turned and led the way. He followed them.

Matthew had stood soundlessly at the edge of the darkening marina and had watched them. He smiled and turned to go. Maybe he thought of his own little sister.

Night Voyage

There were few things that George did poorly, but if he wanted to master something, he did. In high school, he played a trombone so well that he was blackballed by the Musicians Union at the age of seventeen. He was taking gigs away from professional musicians. He built our first television and serviced it for twenty-three years. He was a wonderful teacher and an incredible elementary school principal.

He chose to learn to pilot a boat and used that talent on Yellowstone Lake. For twenty years, he was the Grant Village Boat Patrol Ranger. He drove one of two Bertram boats, a twenty-footer with a small cabin, and a twenty-five-foot boat with a cabin and flying bridge. He did not flee to shore in ten-foot waves, he played in them. He spent thirteen hours a day, five days a week, and both lieu days, on the lake. I, too, loved the lake and the boats.

It was our lieu days and the three of us were to take the twenty-five-foot Bertram eighteen miles south, down lake, to Peale Island. We, George, four-year-old Matthew, and I left Grant Village in the early morning to get ahead of the winds that rose about ten o'clock. Winds would whip up the lake channel, the most dangerous part of the lake. We crossed West Thumb, the first eight miles of the trip. West Thumb is the round, wide and deep extension on the west side of Yellowstone Lake. It is round because It is one of the younger explosion craters within the park, about 174,000 years old.

After crossing West Thumb, we rounded Breeze Point and Sand

Point to travel across the channel. It was relatively easy as we had arrived before the winds. We continued south into South Arm. We slowed down into the no-wake zone. This short four-mile trip adds an hour to the travel time, but slowing down prevents the waves that flood the nests of animals on shore. We stopped at Charcoal Bay where we unlocked one canoe that was cached there for government use. We anchored the Bertram off shore and paddled toward Peale Island.

Matt sat in the middle of the canoe on a flotation seat on the stability bars and wordlessly watched everything. He watched over the gunnels and saw how close to the cold water he sat. He looked up to see the birds, pelicans, mergansers, gulls and bald eagles. He watched the island grow closer. We paddled around to the south side of the island and pulled the canoe up onto shore. He played in the water and explored the island while we worked.

Peale Island cabin was difficult to open. We had the big key for the front door, but it took a long time to remove the thick wooden shutters from the windows. They were secured with heavy iron slide bolts to keep bears out. Without removing some shutters, the cabin was filled with impenetrable darkness. No Coleman lamp could cast enough light to watch a child, or write reports in the cabin log, or cook and clean up after a meal. We needed natural light to see and the wood stove to drive the cold dampness out of the cabin.

Eventually, while George chopped wood and did the outside chores, I cleaned the upper cupboards, the wooden floors in all three rooms and started to clean the lower cupboards. This was where the mouse remains would be found. Mice that have been left dead in a trap for several months are as light as a feather. They look like little gray patches of carpet.

The supper meal had to be big enough to sustain us, so either we had to bring in all of our food in a cooler, or I could cook on the Majestic Range. It was a beautiful stove, but it took talent to cook on it. On the left side, the wood was burned to heat the three-foot wide iron griddle. It heat the water in the giant tea kettle to scald the washed dishes. The Majestic was nine feet tall but it fit into the high kitchen. It did not brush the embossed metal ceiling. Bread was kept warm in the biscuit box above my head and the chimney pipe exited through the roof. Cooking anything was a chore. The Majestic deserved its name, but it took talented cooks to use it properly.

We slept in the bedroom filled with bunks. Army blankets hung heavily from clothes lines strung across the room. Tired little Matthew slept near us, anywhere we put him.

Our stay on the island was never long, but the amount of work that it took to maintain the cabin was great. When it was time to leave, the cabin had to be perfectly clean. The Majestic and the wood stove in the main room had to be rekindled. Matches were left lying close for immediate use. Lastly, the cabin log book had to be brought up to date. Information included the names of those who had come into the cabin, why they were there, what they had done. What we observed needed to be recorded. Finally, everything had to be locked down tight.

Because of all of the work needed to close the cabin, we started late on our trip home. We loaded everything, including bags of garbage, back into the canoe. By the time we reached Charcoal Bay, the temperature was beginning to cool. We pulled and relocked the canoe, re-packed the Bertram, and started to retrace the trip home, north, to Grant Village. One of the great joys of riding in the Bertram was riding up-top, on the flying bridge. George took the wheel on the left and I sat on the right. Matt sat in the middle, up high, so everything could be viewed.

The clear blue night sky was bright with stars, but we could see what the sky ahead held for us. From the north, blackness was rising fast and devouring the stars. We knew we would soon be in total blackness. It was covering the sky like a blanket. We could feel the darkness falling heavily on us. The air cooled, moist and black, like the inside of the cabin. We had a long way to travel in the dark.

George took one last look at any light, set his mental compass and set out for home. But first, he shut off all running lights. They are a distraction. They make it difficult for the eyes to pick up minor reflections on the water. I could not see anything. Sweet Matthew had fallen asleep across my lap. George opened the engine, full bore, and we were up on plane. For miles, we flew in the night, on top of the water that we could not see. We listened to the perfectly tuned engines.

Somehow, George crossed the channel, skirted Breeze Point and Sand Point, and crossed the eight miles of West Thumb. I could not see George beside me nor Matt asleep on my lap. Suddenly, George stopped the boat. I asked him why we stopped. He said, "Because we're home." He took out the spot light from the boat. The light fell exactly between the two metal pilings, the opening to the marina. We were in a perfect triangle, the two pilings and the boat.

I had never heard of anyone who had navigated in total darkness and stopped thirty feet from the entrance to the small Grant Village Marina. George had never questioned his ability to do so. Neither did I.

First Flight

Two American bald eagles had been calling all afternoon. George and I had listened to their plight for at least two hours. The female eagle called from the top of a lodge pole pine tree off to the right of our anchored boat. The male called from straight ahead of the boat. Their calls, chip ... chip ... chip ... chip ... chip ... were loud, clear and urgent. This was unusual for birds that are quiet and watchful. We knew something was upsetting them.

Finally we spied their nest. Their offspring was hopping up and down on the rim of the nest. His wings were flapping, but he was not going anywhere. He reminded me of a teenager, anxious to get out of the door to get his first driver's license.

The parents were calling their young to fly from the nest, to take first flight, to soar with eagles. But the young did not trust his wings. The calling continued. They sounded distressed, but the young one continued with the hopping and flapping and hopping and flapping. With each hop he seemed to say, " I can do this. I can do this. I can do this!"

Suddenly it was quiet. The nest was empty. We looked to the sky for the young eagle, but we could not find him. Then, we saw the male parent on the ground, the nest high above his head. He was in the brush by the shore. His wings were outstretched like a father inviting home his prodigal son. With each hop, he seemed to say, "It's okay. Keep coming, keep coming, keep swimming. You're okay. I'm here."

Junior had not been ready to fly. He had crashed into the cold water and was swimming back to his father. In a near upright position in the water, he used the lower part of his wings as oars to slowly paddle to shore. He looked so bedraggled, so embarrassed, like any teenager whose first attempt at driving had crumpled the car.

Bad Summer

The National Parks of the United States are created for the welfare of the people. They are beautiful, uplifting, and they are for the renewal of souls. But it is the people, the workers of the park, who protect the beauty, the resources, the animals and the visitors.

George was the boat patrol ranger on Yellowstone Lake out of Grant Village one particularly memorable summer. His job was to monitor and protect the southern half of the lake. The rangers and personnel who work the front country are those who cover the ranger station, the visitor center, the campgrounds, power station, maintenance and sanitation. Each usually covers his own job, but often, the lines are blurred.

The roads around Grant Village toward the southern end of the park, are two-lane, with a forty-five mile per hour speed limit. These roads, at that time, were better than many other parts of the park. But, that summer, the road from Grant, south to the Rockefeller Parkway that leads through Teton National Park and into Jackson Hole, was miserable. The road was narrow with hair-pin turns along the Lewis River Canyon. The joke about the size of the pot-holes was that there was a smiling Chinaman waving at us from the bottom of each. At least a car a week broke an axle. The little park service station at Grant Village started to order extra axles. That way, visitors might not have to wait for an axle to be shipped north from Jackson or west from Cody. On this southern road, two vehicles hit the same pot hole at the same time and smashed the others windshield. The station garage could not deal with replacing windshields.

What made the summer worse was, when cars came north to the better road, they sped up, causing more and worse accidents. There were so many accidents or incidents that the rangers were exhausted much earlier in the summer than usual. They were no longer able to cover the area. The ambulance, Lake Hospital, doctors, nurses, and rangers were burned out. One day in particular, George was called in from Yellowstone Lake to assist front country rangers. Toward the close of day, the garbage truck workers took care of the last heart attack victim in the campground.

The summer was not going well. Matthew, nine, and Annie, four, were asleep in the bunk beds in their bed room in our park service trailer called the Commode. That may speak to housing problems and poor morale in the park service, but, George was on the floor in the front room of the trailer, hugging himself, teeth grinding in pain, with his head in my lap. I knew that I could do nothing for him except hold him. I could not leave the children to take him to the hospital. He refused to call for an ambulance because it would disturb already exhausted rangers. We waited until six o'clock when he knew a fresh ranger would come on duty who would take him to the hospital at Lake. He made the call. I found out later that, when George called for the patrol car, the response across Grant Village and the southern half of the park was, "Oh, no. Not George, too!"

George remained at Lake Hospital for three days, sleeping, with a morphine drip until he passed a kidney stone. When I went to pick up George, as was hospital policy, they would not release him until the total bill was paid. They at the desk said, "We take Visa or MasterCard." This was their way of saying that I was not getting him back until the bill was paid in full. Credit cards were new at that time. That was the biggest purchase I had ever made. I felt empowered with a charge card. I could get George back for $996.96. He was worth it. Since George had slept for parts of three days, he looked great. It would be wonderful to have him back at Grant Village by lunchtime, but we did not make it.

A Summer of Heroes

After George passed his kidney stone and was released from Lake Hospital, we put the children safely on the bench seat of our pumpkin-colored Jeep. Along the double-lane road to Grant Village and our trailer, there is an old-growth forest of fir trees, one of the loveliest patches of forest in Yellowstone National Park. We passed the "fir forest" and rounded an up-hill corner where a large "pull off" is located on the opposite side of the road. Pull-offs in the park are constructed for slow traffic to use so faster traffic does not become impatient and pass illegally.

We stopped on the road, bewildered, and stared at the carnage. The road looked like a junk yard. Three cars lay smashed in the left lane. We stopped our Jeep and George stepped out. He had one foot on the pavement when two park visitors who had stopped to help at the crash scene, recognized George's green, NPS ball-cap. They paid no attention to his worn blue jeans and faded t-shirt. They approached him immediately and asked George how the park would want them to proceed. It turned out that the woman was a nurse, the man was a doctor, and they were asking a boat patrolman how to proceed.

Rangers carry their portable radios with them at all times. George sent a call for help to the hospital and all units in the park. George grabbed a notebook. He went from victim to victim. They were scattered on the road, flung into the trees, and in the crushed cars. He, being the first on the scene, triaged the six injured visitors. He wrote down complete identifications and apparent injuries. Rangers arrived. George divided the wounded. He gave the responsibility of each injured party to the person he felt was most qualified to take care of their patient. As more help arrived, more information, vital statistics, from each patient was given to George. It assisted him in a more accurate triage. When he was not writing down information, he was working on the wounded.

Park visitors in cars were trying to pass the accident scene. Suddenly, the park's biggest snowplow with the meanest looking plow blade came around the curve. The plow charged toward the cars approaching from the east. I saw the surprised look on one driver's face. He gave no argument. No driver attempted to pass that park-service-green, deep-V-bladed monster. The plow blocked the road. Cars were stopped from both directions. Drivers turned their vehicles and their plans around.

Visitors were surely inconvenienced and disappointed. Those heading to see Old Faithful were a three-hour drive out of their way. Those heading to Cody, four hours, and, those headed to Jackson Airport for flights, notified the airport that they were on their way. They would get there when they could. Perhaps there were hungry children. Perhaps, this was a once-in-a-lifetime trip to Yellowstone. Perhaps, they would never see Mammoth Hot Springs or the Grand Canyon of the Yellowstone River due to this inconvenience.

I had driven the Jeep with Matthew and Anne to the far side of the pull off. I gave them instructions to stay with the car. They were not to see what was happening. I walked back to the scene, but I could not help with something so above my first aid training.

One of the women involved in the accident had slowly walked, hunched over, to the edge of the pull off and sat in the shade on the concrete curb. I stayed with her. We talked a little. Her eyes did not blink. She was worried about her daughter. Her daughter was "mentally slow" and could not help herself. She would be confused by what was happening. I did not know that George was assisting that girl at that moment. She was severely hurt, unconscious, and George compressed her exposed brain gently back into the base of her skull. We sat for what seemed to be a long time. She did not seem to be badly hurt.

Off to my left, I could see help being given to an unconscious woman who had been flung from her car and into the trees. The silence of the scene will always stay with me. The day had grown warmer and the trees were silent. There was no wind. No one screamed. No one talked above a murmur. Orders, directions, and consultations were spoken quietly and professionally. There was no traffic, no noisy sirens, just a group of people, victims or heroes.

More rangers had arrived, Patty from Old Faithful, Rick from Lake, and rangers unknown to me. Ambulances quietly arrived. Emergency medics tended and loaded those who were hurt. George gave the directions as to who was to be transported first. They left the scene in the order of who was most severely injured. The woman I had stayed with was examined last. She had appeared to me to have few injuries but that was not the case. Rick and Patty examined her. She had sat, slightly slumped over which had been a good thing. The slump had kept the bleeding inside of her to a minimum.

Word had gone out that the west side of the park was closed. There was no traffic to impede the ambulances. Six ambulance runs had been made to the hospital or helicopter "life-flight" pick-up points. They may have been flown to Boulder, CO, or Salt Lake City, Utah. They went to hospitals that could accommodate multiple victims of massive trauma. Three hours of life-saving work had passed. The ambulances, medics, rangers and victims were suddenly gone from the area. George and I retreated to the Jeep and to our children. They had rested or played in the shade of the forest for three hours. They did not ask questions. It was time to leave.

The garage workers within the park had been waiting to clear the wrecked cars from the scene. Usually it is done quickly, not with a three hour wait. Finally, they received permission to clear the roadway. Some of the drivers were young men who enjoyed the thrill of working in Yellowstone National Park, but they were not prepared for the bloody carnage left on the roadway. One young man later mumbled to his fellow garage workers, "It looked like they had been slaughtering hogs." I truly felt badly for him. He did not need to see that.

Only one district in the park had not responded to give aid. But then again, someone had to run the park.

After a few days, George was notified that everyone injured had lived. George had done a superb job of triage, his first and last time. Rangers drive patrol cars, ride horses, and hike alone into bear country. They put out fires and warn children not to lean too far into the waterfalls. They tell visitors what to see and how to get there. It is their duty to pick up garbage, sometimes in full uniform. They direct traffic in bison jams, investigate robberies and arrest the bad guys. Rangers pass physical fitness tests, buy their own uniforms, live in terrible housing, and keep visitors and bears apart. They must qualify with a pistol and a shotgun. George and others were registered EMT's. Do not ever underestimate the courage and abilities of a National Park Service Ranger. Their skills are incredible. They are heroes.

It took several months to put all of the pieces of the accident together. Until those who were hurt were able to be interviewed, the total story was unknown. There had been a fourth vehicle. Instead of using the large pull off on the left, a slow, white motor-home had continued its trek up the hill. The impatient driver behind him could not see around him but tried to pass. As he pulled into the left lane, a car drove over the blind hill. These two cars hit head on with such force that the car coming down the hill flipped upside down and into the air. It crashed down and onto the top of the car traveling behind it. The motorhome continued on its way. It had failed to use the large pull-off provided to keep impatient drivers from attempting to pass illegally. The driver of the motorhome was oblivious to the carnage he had helped to cause.

Diana's Story

Diana and her fifteen siblings were raised Mennonite near the Idaho-Canada border. She met Dwight and they settled in Kansas to farm. There they raised a boy and a girl. They left when Diana's migraines became unbearable. She had become allergic to the fertilizers, insecticides, and herbicides that fill the air and soil. They put their health and happiness ahead of their prosperity.

They worked where they found beauty, in Yellowstone National Park. Diana worked different jobs. Dwight was a big equipment operator. He was handsome, calm, polite and believed in keeping a clean work area. He was a good and stable example for younger employees. Their son was a friend to our son. We all lived in the Grant Village area.

Diana was a pleasure and deeply religious. One summer, she worked at the crowded visitor center information desk. This was a great place for her to work because of her friendliness, patience and knowledge of the park. But she also seemed to possess some sort of sixth sense.

It was a warm day in the Grant Village Visitor Center while Diana was behind the high counter dispensing information. She suddenly felt cold, through and through. She stopped talking and turned to search the eyes of the visitors standing at the desk. She quickly found who had disturbed her. Their eyes locked and Diana felt she was "in the presence of pure evil." She said she could see the depth of this man's evilness. I did not doubt her story. She was not the type of person to be disbelieved and some people seem attuned to the souls of others.

Sometime later in the summer, we just talked. I enjoyed her. Then, I knew she trusted me because she told me her story, perhaps another good reason for them to have left Kansas.

At the time of her story, Kansas was in the news across the country. Nearby ranchers were experiencing cattle mutilations. Cattle, killed in macabre ways, were discovered in farmers' fields without lips, eyes, sex organs and anuses. Most disturbing was the lack of blood. Exsanguination perhaps, done so cleanly that not a drop of blood was found on the ground. No blood was found on the animals as well.

Diana and Dwight had worked a farm raising field crops and owned a small number of cattle. One evening she was alone, which was not all that unusual. She had chores to do in the barn. She collected the pails to feed small calves, but something did not feel right. She did not feel safe in her own barn. It was too still, an unhealthy quiet. The longer she worked, the more disturbed her senses became. She felt there was nothing in the barn to be afraid of, but her mind, body and soul told her that she was in the presence of danger, in the presence of something evil. She continued to work, but she could not console her mind to think that it was just the late hour, just the darkness and lack of stars, just being alone, or a feeling that the air had gone dead.

She resorted to that which had never failed her in the past. Her faith. But this time, her prayer became a deal with God. Her mental conversation went like this. "Dear Jesus, I know I should have no reason to be afraid, but, truly, if I am in danger, spiritually or physically, let me hear an owl hoot." She had not heard an owl hoot in weeks, but in seconds, she heard, not one, not two hoots, but multiple owl hoots from all directions around the barn.

The calf pails flipped from her hands and scattered. She ran to the farmhouse where she turned off all lights so she could not be seen. She locked all doors and windows. She sat in the dark until Dwight arrived home. He asked why everything was so dark. She told him, "Get in the house!" She told him her story of her deal with God and he said, "That's good enough for me."

The cattle mutilations persisted for four years. No one was witnessed, caught or prosecuted for the deeds. The police thought that someone or a few were students at the nearby university. Someone may have been studying the dark arts. Perhaps, after four years, someone had graduated and had left the area because the mutilations stopped as mysteriously as they had begun.

Butt Darts

Some things in life are worth doing and one of those things is butt darts.

We followed the steep trail down to the Snake River by the South Entrance of Yellowstone National Park. Everyone walked, chest deep, across the river except for me. I climbed into the canoe and was deposited on the other side of the river with the backpacks. It was obvious that I could not walk across. Even the tallest trail crew member at six foot five inches had trouble keeping the radio dry. He lifted the radio in his chest harness up to his face as he crossed. They found the river to be deeper than they had thought, and more swift.

Reaching the other side, they put on dry pants, socks and shoes and picked up their overstuffed packs. The crew's packs weighed over sixty-five pounds each. I can pack twenty-four pounds, the weight of one two-year-old child, and I am maxed out. The crew also carried heavy tools, Pulaski axes, in their hands or strapped to the top of their packs. They gave me the toilet paper to carry.

The trail is referred to simply as Six Mile because that is how far it is to hike to the meadow where we were to work. My short legs ran the trail and I panted while their long legs ate up the miles as we traveled through minor ecosystems. We had started through the Juniper that grew in the river gravel. We passed through the lodge pole pine where it had become dryer, and through the meadows filled with prairie grass.

We slid through the slippery black mud where the tall, deep-purple Monkshood grew above my head.

When we arrived at the meadow, it took my breath away. It spread out to the sharp edges of bluffs with pines at the ridge tops. Even in the heat of the warm valley, steam from natural hot spots rose above their rims. Camp had already been set up the previous day by the first half of the trail crew. The only work yet today would be to make something to eat.

We walked two hundred yards to the river to get water. It was not the Snake, but a fast, deep stream with a golden hue. I had the better water filter and their filters were getting clogged with silt so my MSR was appreciated. Some of this water would be boiled and poured into our freeze-dried meal pouches, or drunk as tea, instant coffee, chocolate, or orange Tang. Some of the crew were Mormon and they drank hot Tank. It has long been known as Mormon tea.

I was tired. After camp cleanup, I put up my tent and hoped to rest. We had watched the sky grow dark and threatening. The rain started just as I finished with the tent. I crawled inside and before I had time to remove my hiking boots, lightning lit up the inside of my tent and the thunder cracked, sharp and compressed. The sound fell on us in a heavy wave. We could feel it. It had not traveled far as the lightning had hit the ridge above us.

The meadow was beautiful, but park service horses and mules and visitors' stock animals had contaminated the hot, sunny valley. They had been fed hay that had been packed in on mules. The hay had contained thistles. The seeds fell to the ground from the hay or traveled through the animals that spread the thistles over acres and acres of the valley. These thistles, an invasive variety, took over the valley and every plant had to be eradicated by tools in hand. This was the second year of clearing, but I could not tell that it had ever been touched by a thistle eradication crew.

Clearing thistles is a process. The blossoms at the top must be cut off and collected. They contain the tiny seeds that blow in the wind, so the whole head must be removed. Then, the root must be cut. Usually one good swing with the sharp, flat blade of a Pulaski is all it takes to sever the plant from the root. When thousands of plants are severed, it means thousands of times to lift the heavy Pulaski over-head to swing the axe. It is back breaking work. The plant is left on the ground where it had grown. Eventually, it turns gray, dusty, and each leaf with its threatening thorns looks evil.

We worked for hours. My face grew red. I was not getting enough water to drink. The hot wind dehydrated us, but these thistles were a great source of moisture for insects, especially earwigs. Thousands of them. I hate earwigs with their threatening pincers and shiny brown, quick-moving exoskeletons. They are just ugly. They also were at the right height to meet me in the face as I started to cut off the blossoms. I never knew if I had them in my hair or down my shirt. Their name, earwig, implies that they crawl into one's ears. I have had enough of earwigs for a lifetime.

As I worked, I came to a hot river. It gushed with the rush of a hot fire hydrant. It was superheated, above the boiling point, and dangerous. The hot river was only six feet long. It exited the earth as if shot from a pipe. It was a foot across, arched six inches above the ground and plunged into a hole below a small mound of prairie grass. I had never seen anything like it, or so dangerous, in any other thermal basin in the park. I no longer trusted the ground I was standing on and proceeded with great caution.

I went back to camp for a rest and a drink when I noticed a bighorn sheep ram on the other side of the golden river. His hide glowed red in reflected sunlight. His great curved horns nearly encircled each side of his huge head. I had never seen an animal so stunning.

It was time for the crew to quit for the day. We cooked, ate and cleaned the camp. It was too early to retire to sleep so we did what people have done for centuries, we entertained ourselves. Bill was the life of every party. He always had something funny to say or do, so he taught us how to play butt darts. First, he told us that we were never to tell anyone about the game. We are now past that time. Then he collected a small handful of coins from anyone who had then. Coins have little value in the back country, but not tonight.

This is how the game is played. Someone, hopefully someone with a big foot, contributes a shoe. Just one. This serves as a repository for coins. The first player stands behind the starting line about fifteen feet away from the shoe. The stack of coins is deposited as far up into the rectal area as one can push. The butt muscles are clamped tightly to keep the coins in place. The player then walks from the starting line to the shoe. Positioning oneself over the shoe, and with a sudden thrust squat, coins are hopefully deposited into the shoe. The one with the most coins in the shoe, wins.

But, before one gets to the shoe, traveling this short distance can be difficult. It is not natural to walk with butt muscles tightly constricted. The body becomes contorted. It results in a strange way of walking. It can result in a tinkling of coins being released down the pant leg. Getting into position over the shoe to release the remaining coins onto a target is more like a WWII bombing run. Then, bombs away!

I did well, but there is always someone better. Jan was younger and a good athlete. No one was going to see her waddle to the shoe. No way! She cart-wheeled the 15 feet, stuck the landing over the shoe, and deposited the coins with the fastest squat we had ever seen. In competitive Olympic terms, it was a ten. The prospect of having created an arc of coins, flung to the sky, had been more than possible. How did she not lose the coins? We conceded that she had won. We did not bother counting the coins.

We slept hard that night. We still had a half of a day to work on the thistles and a half of a day to hike out. The plan had been to collect the blossoms, bag them, and carry them out. We contacted the front country by radio and let them know that we could not carry out over 300 pounds of thistle blossoms. They told us that horses would be brought in to remove the bags of seeds in a few days.

It was time to leave this beautiful valley that few people get the opportunity to see. The head of this thistle clean-up project was one of the strongest women I have ever met. I was given extra weight to carry out, but nothing like the amount of gear that Bridgette carried. Her pack weighed at least eighty pounds. She put flip-flops on her feet and led the way out and down the trail. She knew that if she wore her boots, she would suffer greatly. The pressure and heat inside the boot builds like a pressure cooker. It causes the toe nails to turn black.

Walking out on a trail that has been hiked from the other direction so recently is like a movie reel rewinding. Your mind's eye wants to continue to face the beauty of the valley, but the trail must be watched to avoid falling, especially with a heavy pack. The mind then keeps one view of the valley permanently in the back of the mind, and the reel goes backwards. We stepped into the woods. We remembered the prairie meadow, the black earth, and the purple Monkshood, in deep shadow this time.

We passed through the Lodge pole pine, the Juniper, and the river. After the six miles we could see the vehicles. Vehicles mean "civilization." It means the sad and abrupt end of the contact of your footfalls upon the earth. It means talking. The silence of the trail is a gift of grace. It is a physical and mental let-down to remove a heavy pack after suffering in beauty. It is an anti-climactic end to hiking into the back country.

Orion

Orion charged 'ore the mountains from the East
And stalked to my window while fast asleep
And woke me to the cold to see the golden seven.

I raced the stairs in night-gown wear
and threw the door open wide; he was there,
beyond wonder, burning lesser stars from the sky.

Dominance of the night came from the heights of Betelgeuse
to the blue-diamond gleam of Rigel.
The pinched in waist of the thee-starred belt
proved warrior lean and hardened.

The Giant Hunter, no handsomer star formation,
he stands, with bow in hand, to chase the Pleiades
'round the heavens.

Heart thumping and breath forgotten,
entranced with astral awe, I was Lot's wife turned to stone,
'til snowy bare feet forced my retreat
from the wonder that is the warrior.

Twenty-Seven Seconds

It was late May and George and I had returned to Yellowstone from Michigan, like migrating birds for the 30th summer. The weather was easily defined as "yucky." At an elevation above 7,000 feet, the park would be wet for another two weeks. Everything was gray. There is so much snow to melt that the water rises, visibly in the air. The snow had only recently melted at the sides of the road that wound through the Hayden Valley.

Roads in Yellowstone take a beating from the severe cold of winter and ten to twenty feet of heavy snow. The road-beds are subjected to severe frost heaves. The road's surface is soft because the space between the gravel stones has deteriorated. It leaves the gravel separated from the tar that should hold it together. It resembles a moving gray path of slightly-spongy, wet cornstarch. The heat of the sun and the wear of tires melts the gravel and tar back together when July and the tourists arrive.

I see what is going on around me in terms of numbers. I count anything, not just pills in my hand or steps on the stairs. I count the number of times I pull the handle on the flour sifter and the number of seconds I let the water run to flush the pipes or fill the tea kettle.

We were heading south from Canyon Village, through the Hayden Valley, to Lake Village. The road was soft. The edges of the road had unraveled like a poor, ancient weaving. My mental count began as the back-right tire fell off the highway at a place where the road had been undercut. The road's white guide line had disappeared off the edge into a long muddy pond.

The second second, the tire exploded. The next four seconds, we rode on the axle on the road while trying to stop. Second number six, George managed to get the wheel back onto the road, but the flat tire was an anchor that dragged on the road. In seconds seven, eight and nine, George fought to keep us in the right lane. Seconds number ten through fifteen were do-or-die.

In the twenty-three-mile valley, we had not met one car, when out of the nearing dusk, an older model purple van approached. We were heading for an angled front-to-side collision. I saw the lovely face of the woman in the passenger seat who was watching me. I could feel that the van was filled with lovely, blond children. Only feet separated our vehicle from their side when George wrenched the steering wheel to the right.

In second sixteen, we headed back toward the ditch on the right. George torqued the wheel left but that put the back right wheel off of the road again where we rode for seconds seventeen and eighteen. At nineteen, the right front wheel fell off the edge of the roadway. We rode on the skid-pan, two wheels on and two wheels off, for what seemed like an eternity. I placed my two hands around George's upper arm to let him know that, no matter what happened next, we would do it together as we had for the previous forty years.

I had not spoken during this entire time, but at second number 23, I quietly said, "We are going to roll." Well, that was obvious. We were already rolling over, slowly and gently, but to what end?

At second 24, George saw what could save us, a rocky culvert mound. George muscled an 80-degree right turn, launching us onto the mound. The flat tire hit the edge of the concrete culvert. We later realized that that had righted the car and we were no longer going to roll over, but it also moved the entire right side of the car backwards, two inches off the frame. We scraped and jolted down the rocks and gravel of this short incline. Parts of the car were ripped off and flung wide. I could hear them and saw them fly. At second 26, we hit the mud and the snow-melt with a "fwoop." At second 27, we spun left and the car stopped.

Funny, I guess. But we did not ask each other if we were okay. We eyed each other and knew we were unhurt. Our fate had been held in 27 seconds.

That someone had "rolled their car" was reported to rangers at Canyon Village. The lovely people in the purple van came back to assist us. The next three weeks were ones of bad weather, rental cars, insurance claims, and all that made for a time of inconvenience. We counted our blessings.

A Spider's Web

Summer was officially over in Yellowstone National Park. The thermometer on the rear-view mirror of the Tahoe read eight degrees. I scraped the ice from the windshield and climbed into the cold that permeated the car. It was before 6 a.m. That gave me over an hour to take photos before I had to be back at the apartment. George would need a good breakfast before working in the cold all day.

I drove west into the Hayden Valley toward Mud Volcano, a place of wandering hot pots, deep fissures, shallow hot pools and belching Dragon's Mouth. I wanted to take pictures of the frost that might have formed near the hot features. I knew the valley would be filled with thick fog. The river was giving up its heat.

But before Mud Volcano, I would make other stops to take photographs. I tell people that I take pictures of anything that either moves or doesn't move. It would be good to practice with my new camera.

As I had predicted, fog was thick along the river road. I could not see any oncoming lights so I cautiously crossed onto the paved pull-off on the south side of the road. I saw nothing, but I could hear the slight sound of the bison herd moving through the frozen weeds and along the river, so I waited. They were coming my way. Very few minutes passed before I could see the first two dark v-shaped heads appearing out of the fog. They were a long way off.

The flat angle of the sun turned the fog to a soft sepia, like artists who sketch a small, far-away old scene and let your mind fill in the rest. The bison were moving fast. I could see their backs and the curly locks of hair between their horns. They were covered in frost from the humidity from the river, and from their own breath.

More bison appeared. I took several pictures, but I needed to retreat to the warm car. Taking pictures in such bitter cold is tough on camera batteries, and tough on the photographer. My fingers were white and bloodless though they had been covered with gloves.

I carefully exited the pull off. I made a few hurried stops along the way, but I was excited at the prospects of what I would see at Mud Volcano. Frost forms by the belching caverns, hot swamp, pools, grasses and flowers that still live beside the heat.

Mud Volcano had other photographers there this morning. It was a photographers' paradise. The sun's rays seemed to know what they were supposed to do. They fell on the pool near Dragon's Mouth Cauldron whose belched heat instantly condensed into an ever-thickening fog. Hoar frost crystals grew anywhere they could. For twenty minutes of awe, I captured the rays of light that glittered or lit up the colors in the hot water holes in the shallow pool. I shot the yellow monkey flowers and the green spikes of grasses. They survived in the geyser heat on such a bitter, cold day.

And there it was, the picture that would light up my mind forever. A spider's web was strung between two tall green grass spikes. Each web strand glittered with hoar frost above the warm water and into the icy air. Each strand was a fourth of an inch wide with frost. It was perfect. The strands were set wide apart like the web drawn in white frosting on a dark Halloween cake. It was the lines drawn in the corners of the pages of *Charlotte's Web.*

I needed to watch my time but it was the bitter cold that shoved me back into the car. With the poor visibility, I watched the parking lot for people, cars, and animals. I watched for slick spots on the narrow curvy road. I slowed for the heavy drifts of fog as they crossed the road from the hot geyser features. And, of course, I watched for more animals. No one wins in a collision with a one-ton bison.

I was headed home, but each time I warmed up, the temptation was there to stop to see more and "practice" with my camera. So, I pulled off the road again. I knew exactly where I was in the fog. I parked on the pull off site where I knew the river passed within ten feet of where I would park.

This was the widest part of the river so the water was only inches deep. The water was nearly still so ice was forming on the edges, but the crystals were not special and did not warrant a picture. I walked a short distance along the river checking the edges when I heard it.

It was the warning rumble of a bull bison. He was somewhere and close. The fog absorbed the rumble so the warning had come from all directions. I looked up. The most logical place for him to be would be between the pull off and the river to the east of me. I did not dare to move quickly. The worst thing for me to do would be to run and take the chance of charging into him.

The second rumble came. I know nothing about music, but my theory is that, the age, weight and possible health of a bull bison can be told by the pitch of the rumble. This was an ever so slightly higher pitch. This bull sounded young as though it did not yet have its full growth and weight. Young bulls are unpredictable. Still, a bull rumble is the deepest, most threateningly beautiful, melodic base sound in the animal kingdom. I thought, musicians could take a lesson from bull bison.

I looked for any dark shape in the fog. He had warned me twice so it was time to move up the short slope to the pull-off and the car. I moved slowly as I did not want to stumble and startle him. In the white fog I could see my whiter car and I walked toward it. I never saw any other shape.

It was time to go back to the apartment. I was hungry.

I walked into the apartment and George was dressed. His green jeans and gray uniform shirt looked warn out. They had lasted the summer work season. He was seated, putting on his boots and getting ready for a very cold day.

As usual, I started to tell him about the pictures I had taken at Mud Volcano. Also, as usual, I moved into the warmth of his aura. He was always twice my size and I loved his warmth. I slightly rested my weight on his knee and handed my camera to him. I wanted him to see the spider web.

The camera was new to both of us and I asked him a technical question about it. George was my guru, my hero with cameras, computers and all demonic things electric. He started to look, but, without words, the mistake was made. He deleted the memory chip. All pictures were gone. He did not move. We just looked at the camera. I moved to face him, placed my hands lightly on his shoulders and kissed his very high tanned forehead. I looked into the brown eyes that had won me thirty-eight years previously and said, "What would you like with your sausage? Cereal or eggs?"

The Beaver Ponds

I had paid for the right to hike with a National Park Service ranger and others along the Beaver Ponds Trail. I waited for the hike to begin at the Hoo Doos located south of Mammoth Hot Springs, Yellowstone National Park. The Hoo Doos are large rocks, weather-warn and rounded. They had broken from the massive layer of limestone eight-hundred feet above. Rocks still break from the parent layer and tumble down into piles.

The hiking group formed. We listened to the greeting and explanation from the ranger. Immediately I wondered if I could keep up with this long-legged and energetic young man.

The first upward pitch was only fifty feet, but it put us on a trail into acres of white Labrador Tea bushes growing along the steep slope. They are deceptively poisonous, but they were glorious. The day was beautiful and the sun lit up the tiny white petals. I took a few pictures and scooted to catch up with the rest of the group. Every few feet I found something else that was new to me. I would stop to take a picture, or two. I would look up and see the last hiker going out of sight and I would run to catch up to the group. No one wants to be last on a trail in bear country.

This progressed for a couple of miles. Each time I caught up with the group, they had already stopped, rested and were ready to begin again. I had not had time to take a drink. This repeated several times.

We hiked over a hill that descended into a narrow valley with a small stream. The trail switch-backed down the hill to five gray, dusty logs that served as a bridge. At the base of the hill I came upon a rabbit brush plant in full bloom. The leaves and stems reflected olive green and silver. The fine, spiky-haired yellow flowers were golden in the sun. It was covered with butterflies taking nectar. I was so in awe that my mouth gaped and I yelled at the last person to come and see what I was seeing. He looked back at me as if he were escaping an ax murderer and he ran.

A breeze disrupted the six-foot diameter yellow bush. In the bright sunshine, the bush erupted into a mass of yellow butterflies, all sizes with flashes of gold, orange and brown. My eyes popped and my brain became indelibly imprinted with vibrating yellow. I wanted to stay there until I had taken a picture of each of them, but instead, I ran.

When I caught up with the group, they were disgusted with me. I received ornery comments. They started giving me snacks to "give me more energy." Not one of them spoke of unusual beauty. None had seen the burning bush in the desert.

I tried to stay closer to the group, passing by wonderful things that I wanted to investigate. We finally took a long break on the widest part of Beaver Creek known as the Beaver Ponds. The ranger said there had not been one beaver sighted there in a quarter of a century. There was nothing there of interest to warrant a picture.

The hike ended. It just ended. There were no comments as to what a great trail it had been or what wonderful things they had seen. Why did they hike the trail? To say they could hike a few miles in Yellowstone National Park? In record time? The hike was not the one I had wanted or expected; the hike I had taken was not one the other hikers had taken either.

One Never Hikes Alone

One never hikes alone, but park rangers do. They go where they want and return with stories of brightly lit waterfalls in the back country, uncharted geyser basins with blue pools, and Peregrine falcon nests with chicks. I could do that, if I were not afraid of hiking alone. I love to hike, but each time I hiked in Yellowstone National Park, it seemed to involve an encounter with a grizzly bear in some dangerous way.

A very short trail runs along the Yellowstone Lake outlet. This small beautiful flow of water becomes the Yellowstone River, running north to the Missouri River, east to the Mississippi River and into the Gulf of Mexico. That little outlet trail called my name, over and over again, to investigate it. It was an unusual view. A wildflower meadow was at the end of the trail. I felt compelled to hike the trail, but I cringed.

One restless morning, I drove to Fishing Bridge and parked in the large, new parking lot. I crossed the road to the twenty steps that led up the hill to the trail. I told myself that I could hike a half-mile trail alone in Yellowstone and I would survive nicely. It would do wonders for my bravery. After that, I could do other hikes alone.

The trail was on a thirty-foot-high bluff in dry prairie grass. A narrow line of Lodge Pole pine trees grew on my left, between me and the lake outlet at the base of the bluff.

Not one-third of a mile onto the trail, I stopped. I could not force one foot to pass in front of the other. Something deep within me told me to stop. It was more than an eerie quiet, it was silence. I envisioned every little bird holding its song. Every little critter was stopping in his tracks, listening and dashing for its den. The hair on the back of my neck raised. I turned around and double-timed it back down the trail to the steps.

I felt a little shaken. I was disappointed in myself. From the top step, I looked down at the road. George's boss, Barbara, was greeting visitors and answering the typical tourist questions like, "When the sun goes down, does it get dark here?" and "When do the deer turn into elk?" We exchanged greetings, but I was in a hurry to retreat to my vehicle. Why was I so afraid to hike alone?

At the end of the day, George came home for dinner. I greeted him at the door as always, but I did not ask him how his day went. I was going to confess to him that a little, unfinished, hike had upset me. But I never said a word because he spoke too quickly. "Wait until I tell you what happened to Barbara today! You know where the steps are at Fishing Bridge where it leads to the outlet trail?"

Yes! I knew exactly where the steps were. Right where I had last seen Barbara.

George said, "Judy, you won't believe this! Barbara walked the outlet trail this afternoon. She only hiked in less than a half of a mile when she saw a disturbance between the trail and the bluff. She approached the ruckus to see what it was. A huge grizzly pulled his blood-drenched head out of the abdomen of an elk he had just killed. He stood on his hind legs, red shoulders dripping, and challenged her." George said Barbara instinctively made her mental apology to the bear and stopped approaching. She lowered her head and eyes and softly walked backwards to the trail.

Barbara was smart and had survived the encounter. She had done everything correctly to avoid challenging the grizzly. She had nearly walked into a bad situation. But I also had avoided the grizzly encounter. I had felt and heard the changes in the sounds around me. If I had continued to hike, I am convinced that the bear would have taken me instead of the elk. It was a strong instinctual reaction toward self-preservation. For that, I am thankful.

The Cutthroat Trout Story

Off Breeze Point in Yellowstone Lake, I carefully reeled in the oversized, glittering, copper-colored cutthroat trout. This trout would be one of the last large ones in the lake because it was too large to be eaten by lake trout and illegal to be kept. I did not pull the cutthroat out of the water for fear of hurting the fish, so there is no photo of me holding up an eight-pound cutthroat trout. It was sad that so few cutthroat remained in the lake. Their demise is one of the greatest ecological disasters in the United States.

I have my own opinion of why this disaster occurred. It has been studied extensively by scientists from outside of the park, but my ideas have come from observation and listening to people who have had a long contact with the lake. This is the non-scientific version.

In 1952, it is said that the park wanted a larger, sportier, fish that was more difficult to catch, would fight harder and had to be reeled up from a greater depth. That is when the lake trout were stocked in the lake. But, to the park's disappointment, they failed to thrive. For the next fifty years, it was claimed by a few fishermen that they had caught a lake trout. Since the fish would have been oversized, the evidence, the fish itself, would have been returned to the lake as per fishing regulations. Some fishermen left Bridge Bay Marina in a sour mood when they were told they were mistaken. Those at the Bridge Bay back-country office with less knowledge about fish, told experienced fishermen there were, absolutely, no lake trout in Yellowstone Lake.

The change from catching cutthroat to lake trout was a shock. Suddenly, no legal cutthroat were being caught. The reason had started several years after the great Fires of '88. Fires in the park had been suppressed for decades. Smokey the Bear told us that fires were bad and were to be prevented. For decades, the litter on the forest floors lay unburned. In some places, it was nine feet deep. But Mother Nature taught us many lessons in 1988.

The spring of 1988 was wet. Grasses and shrubs grew rapidly and abundantly. When the rains stopped, everything dried out quickly. Summer stormed brought in little rain to put out any fires that were started by lightning strikes. There was a feeling of dread in the park that summer. Rangers felt the park would burn. That, if the fires started, they would have so much fuel, the fires would be impossible to stop. Rangers were correct, but they had more to fear than they thought. Many fires started in July and they did not stop burning until September 6th when a heavy snow storm and cool weather arrived.

Over one third of the park had burned and that is the reason for the loss of cutthroat trout. The trees and the soil were so badly burned that tons of ash were created. Ash is filled with the nutrients that had been bound up in the forests for decades. Grasses no longer had contained the nutrients that animals needed to be healthy. Deer were observed licking ash from smoldering logs to acquire the nutrients they craved. These nutrients ran into the "nutritionally deficient" Yellowstone Lake. Lake trout started to flourish with the added nutrients that fell to the bottom of the lake where lake trout live. Cutthroat are top feeders. They live off the bugs at the top of the lake. They did not benefit from the new nutrients.

The fires were so intense that the soil burned deeply, down to the sand and rock. When the rains came, there was nothing to prevent the landslides that occurred throughout the park. The mud ran to the rivers. Sediments covered the insects at the bottoms of streams where brook trout, grayling and other fish live. These sediments were then carried by every stream to the lakes. Yellowstone Lake has over a hundred small streams that empty into it. A massive quantity of ash and sediment washed into the lake. It added nutrients, but it also covered the eggs of the cutthroat that were deposited at the mouths of the streams.

Lake trout were rapidly reproducing, growing, and eating the smaller cutthroat. Legal cutthroat disappeared from the lake and the fishermen complained. Eggs of the bigger cutthroat were either eaten by lake trout or silted over at the stream mouths. The cutthroat population "crashed" and reproduction dwindled to a halt.

For deep-water fishermen, this seemed great. Some of the lake trout caught were over thirty pounds. But the disaster was not fully recognized until forty-three species that depended upon the cutthroat trout began to disappear from the lake. The most obvious losses were the eagles and osprey that had caught the cutthroat that lived in the upper layer of the water. The lake became silent. Huge, unused eagles' nests crashed down from the trees. Osprey were observed hunting snakes on the land. Other large birds like pelican and blue heron suffered. The bears devised new ways and locations to acquire protein because there were no fish in the streams. Bears began eating elk calves to make up for the lack of protein previously supplied by fish. One summer, not one elk calf was known to have survived in the Lake Village area. Ecological balance had been destroyed.

An expensive campaign was begun to destroy the lake trout. A trawler from the Great Lakes was brought to the lake and a crew was hired. Hundreds of thousands of lake trout have been caught in nets, killed, and returned back into the lake. This is tons of fish that cannot be given away or sold to eat. They contain high concentrations of heavy metals that are found in the lake. These minerals come from volcanic fumeral vents at the bottom of Yellowstone Lake. The huge increase in biomass of the dead fish that were dumped back into the lake has created masses of fat, overfed leeches. The lake trout then ate the leeches because the cutthroat are gone. The lake trout, with so much to eat, have become overpopulated. They are now smaller in size and less desirable for sports fishermen to catch.

A natural comeback for the beautiful cutthroat is impossible. The gorgeous lake is ruined. We have touched more than just one edge of the spider's web; we have torn the entire web of life. It is an ecological disaster, unable to be repaired.

Ashes

There was a beautiful Mass, planned exactly the way I wanted it. Music played and Biblical passages were read that fit exactly who he was. "Consider the lilies of the field …" Songs were strong with references to nature. The final hymn was "America the Beautiful." People cried. I kissed George's casket one last good-by.

The luncheon followed. Each food was perfect. The widow was going through all the social paces. After all, I am Mrs. George W. Monroe. Widow. I wore a new black suit. This was not being done for me. It was for him. It was done in his memory. My conduct and decisions would be his final standing.

What a terrible word, widow. It implies that everything is left to do by the one left behind. I had hundreds of thank-you cards to send to those who sent Mass cards, sympathy cards, good-wishes and flowers. I listened to visitors' stories that renewed their tears for George. But I did not cry. Crying takes too much energy. I had started grieving so long before George died that tears did not matter.

It had been ten months that George's cremains, bagged in plastic in a black box, had been on the fireplace mantle. I packed them into my luggage. The box contained the certificate of authenticity making it legal to travel with what had once been a big, handsome, husband. My children had convinced me to return to Yellowstone National Park. I did not want to go. It seemed to be too early. I suggested waiting another year. My children argued against waiting. Sometimes, you let others make decisions. You are too tired to care what decisions are made.

I met up with my children, Matt and Anne, Matthew's wife, Carrie, and my one-year old grand-daughter, Kora Mae. From Jackson Hole, Wyoming, we traveled to a special potluck in Lake Village, Yellowstone National Park. It had been set up in honor of George. All of George's friends and bosses were there. Several had driven for three hours from Bozeman, MT, where they lived. It was truly a sacrifice for them to be there. They had brought great food and placed it on the mess-hall tables. It was a large group and all chairs were filled.

I did not know the guests well, but George had worked with them every day. After eating, George's fellow boat patrol ranger, Rick, stepped in front of me wearing his boat patrol uniform. He is a handsome man but he did not look good. I thought he was going to pass out, so I grabbed him and said, "Rick, you look great in a uniform." I had hoped to break the tension with levity and save him from falling over and embarrassing himself, but I do not think his bosses appreciated my conduct. He was about to present to me the triangularly folded flag given to the loved ones of military heroes. One does not interrupt the presentation of the United States flag. He made it through the salute and handed to me the folded flag. I had not known what was going on. No seasonal National Park Service ranger that I had ever heard of had received the military flag and salute. It was an incredible honor. George deserved it. I had not been expecting it.

The following morning, Matt, Anne and I met Rick at the Bridge Bay Marina at nine o'clock. I carried the cremains. I knew every inch of where we would travel. We were heading down the eighteen-mile long lake to spread George's ashes on and around Peale Island, George's favorite place on earth.

The official law enforcement boats with lights, paint and banners were too big or used too much gasoline to make the trip. Also, they would not comfortably hold the four of us. Therefore, we were taking the Frog, the mid-sized maintenance boat. I loved the Frog. The Frog was a twenty-eight-foot aluminum work boat with a cabin standing in the middle of the deck. It had a passage on each side between the cabin and the gunnels. If one needed a heavy job to be done, one sent for the Frog. I felt comfortable here.

The morning felt non-descript. It was not hot, not cold, not sunny nor foggy. It was just there. No smiles appeared on any pair of lips. We left the maintenance area of Bridge Bay Marina. We traveled out and under the bridge with the prescribed rpm's so as not to create a wake. Just past the last buoy, Rick put the Frog up on plane. We passed Sand Point, Stevenson's Island, Dot Island, and passed the most dangerous part of the lake, the channel. It was still early enough so no wind had ruffled the surface of the lake. Again, non-descript. It was a rare day that the lake lacked personality. The first eight miles had been easy and had taken less than an hour of travel time.

As we approached Plover Point, we centered the Frog into the middle of the South Arm of Yellowstone Lake. The arm is a mile wide and six miles long. We slowed to a no-wake speed in the Arm. This second part of the journey would take an hour. It always did. In the spring, the shores of the South Arm were filled with bird's nests, chicks and eggs. The nests were being flooded by visitors in fast boats, so the no-wake zone had been devised and enforced. The law was working. It was a slow but pleasant journey on the lake in the morning.

Arriving at Charcoal Bay, a small horseshoe shaped spit, we approached the shallow shoreline. The front-loading ramp of the Frog was lowered. Three Monroe's walked off. Rick unlocked two canoes from on shore that are seasonally left there for park service business. From the bay, we would finish the trip by canoe. Rick loaded one canoe on the Frog, pulled away from shore, and anchored a short distance away in deeper water. He returned in the canoe. We secured the lunch cooler in one canoe, grabbed the paddles, and donned our lifejackets. I set the cremains at my feet. We paddled for Peale Island cabin, but we skirted the bay around the southern shore of South Arm. We did not paddle straight for the cabin. Those who know Yellowstone Lake, never trust her. Deadly winds arrive in an instant. George always referred to Yellowstone Lake as "a pretty lady with teeth." One could not survive her cold waters.

We paddled for an hour before arriving at the southern end of Peale

Island. Near the mouth of Monument Creek, we stopped. Everything was quiet and the water was still. I opened the cremains. Our two canoes were side by side. I handed the dipper to Rick. He said, "Are you sure you want me to go first?" I was sure, only because I did not want to be first, nor did I want Annie to start crying. I did not want Matt to remember that he would be first to commend his father's gray ashes into the lifeless, gray water. So we began.

Each of us used the dipper to spread the ashes into the water that George loved so much. These were the waters he protected day and night, above and beyond the call of duty, without hesitation. When the dipper came to me, I had nothing profound to say. No great words of love exited my mouth. My lips were tight and smile-less. I kept the rest of the ashes for myself to distribute on the island.

We paddled to the tiny cove in front of the cabin. It was always a strange, exciting feeling to step foot on Peale island. George was here. I could feel him. The island was barely three feet in elevation but green and lush in places, with tall Lodge Pole pines. The sandy bottom had three inches of water where the canoes were brought in. Sometimes when the water was high in the spring, the island would be cut into two very small islands. Today it was one.

The others took the cooler of food to set up the lunch on the picnic table. But first, they would open the cabin doors, but not open the cabin. Opening the cabin entailed removing the heavy wooden window shutters with the wrought iron struts. The place looked as familiar as the day that George and I made our first trip in, over thirty years ago.

Annie and I stepped into the trees and talked softly about my plans to walk the island. In a heartbeat, a Great Grey owl flew from a low tree branch. Annie automatically ducked. It flew away, flying lowly, slowly and gracefully through the pines. It was a reminder of the beauty that George had shared with us in the national parks. It was an owl's fly-by tribute to a man who had protected them.

I left Annie and took the dipper and the ashes. It weighed about eight pounds and I decided to give the island a good Baptism. I headed for the front of the cabin. The island had been washing away and more bare tree roots were exposed than on my last visit. It was here that

George had stood and made sixteen casts and caught sixteen beautiful oversize cutthroat trout. He had released them all. I placed ashes there with a silent blessing for the colorful cutthroat trout that had once lived in the lake but were now gone.

I walked to where the historic outhouse had been. It, too, was gone, but my memories were not. The outhouse had been perfectly located so you could look up lake for ninety miles to the top of Mt. Washburn. It was such a beautiful view and the outhouse was so close to the water that no one bothered to close the door while doing business. On one trip, I remembered that the men, George and his boss, were going to dig a new trench in the hard, volcanic soil. My job on that trip had also concerned the outhouse.

Over the winter, Agape spiders had decided the outhouse would be a great place to live. Every inch, top to bottom, was filled with thick webs. Spiders hung like Christmas tree decorations. Since, on that day with the men, I had been allowed to ride along in the park boat, I got to clean the spiders. One spider is fine, but I was greatly outnumbered. They were above my head by three feet and all the way down to my shoes. First, I threw water on them. That was dumb. It only alerted the spiders to my intention to bring them down. Sticks were too short and the webs were too thick and gummy. The broom was too short and flimsy and the spiders really freaked me out.

While I was afraid that spiders would run up my pant legs, I heard the giggles of two grown men I think they had finally thought it through. What they were doing was stupid. They were never going to get the hole dug. What I was doing was also stupid. Just bring down the spider webs with a canoe paddle and run. Duh! Those foolish thoughts made me laugh for the first time since George had become sick. What was wrong with me?

I crossed the moss-covered six-foot causeway that held the island together and walked the trail into the woods. I reached the place where I had been attacked years ago by a grouse. She meant business and I did not feel like explaining grouse scratches on me for the rest of the summer. She would not let me pass on the trail. I knew I had to be near her nest because she was, what, "Madder than a wet hen"? I had had my camera with me so I used the flash. She stopped momentarily with each flash, but then attacked me again. I flashed the camera four times before I worked my way past her. I left extra ashes there for the pink flowers that grew there. I gave ashes in memory of a protective mother grouse.

The island had been used for park personnel for many years and for many reasons. Back-country rangers used it on their patrols. It was there for those who needed the silence of its remoteness. There were those, such as I, the wife, who tagged along to clean the cabin. But, over time, things changed when head rangers from Mammoth found it to be a great place to entertain Congressmen. They packed the boat deck with food and disappeared into the back country. It was great fun for them to stay at the cabin and tour the lake. However, sanitation had become a problem. Something had to be done.

It took all too little planning, but one day the black-box throne arrived. The Bertram had been used to float the sealed organic toilet from Grant Village, across the Thumb, across the channel, through the no-wake zone, and into the hand propelled zone. It was set adrift at the tiny mouth of the tiny island bay. The black plastic, bio-mass toilet vault was floated the last hundred feet of water. When it touched the lake bottom. the attempt was made to haul it onto the unleveled volcanic ground. Eventually, it was left at a bad angle, partly in and partly out of the the water.

To use this new facility, one needed to climb the five feet up to the top of the toilet vault and onto the toilet seat. The bad angle meant that, while sitting on the throne, hanging onto the toilet seat was like trying to stay on a bucking steer in a rodeo. Just to add one more insult, with the six feet of increased elevation, a person sitting on the throne, was fully visible to everyone from the front porch of the cabin.

I had to keep from laughing aloud. The flood of thoughts continued. Right out there was where three-year old Annie had fallen out of the canoe and cried because we had to return to the cabin for dry clothes. She wanted to be on the water and getting dry was a waste of time to her. Once, a tree had been blown down close to Anne. She screamed like a banshee.

Matt, where were you? You were always so quiet and rarely in trouble. You slept so soundly in the car seat at my feet when we canoed into the cabin for the first time. We put you safely in a dresser drawer on the floor to sleep at night. You were always where my hand could touch you.

We had found a "mouse penthouse" in the fire wood closet. It had been chewed from a fresh, unused mop. It was a perfect and pleasant piece of mouse architecture. The kitchen is where I had grudgingly cleaned up the cans of botulistic green beans that had exploded in the cupboard over the winter. It was where I cooked on the beautiful Majestic range that was heated with kindling wood. It had a covered metal cupboard and a biscuit keeper. The stove lived up to its name for it majestically reached to the high ceiling.

From the front window, a pelican, bathed in gold morning light, had coasted over the lake in an eternally untaken photograph. The first time I had ever seen a complete rainbow was here. This is where George wanted to live during the Fires of '88 no matter how preposterous the idea. It was my decision that we were blessedly not working in the park that summer. For the well-being of our family, I will never regret that decision.

I covered the island in a fog of ashes. I did not give ashes to family members in little bottles nor did I save them to place elsewhere. That would have haunted me. I knew where every part of George belonged. Then I looked at my clothing. I was covered in powdery George-ash, head and hair, face and sweatshirt. I was not disgusted by the idea. It was a George touch good-by, thanking me, and including me in his happiness. I brushed off the ashes gently as if not to disturb them, not to push him away from his embrace. I caught myself relaxing, smiling, my teeth unclenching. I had done my duty. I knew exactly where he was, where he would always be, and where he had always wanted to be. I had brought him home.

Gandhi

Stew had worked for forty-five years in the National Park Service. The last twenty years had been in Grand Canyon National Park where he became Chief Naturalist. In college, he had studied literature. He was the only man I have ever known to display a gold embossed set of the complete works of Shakespeare. He used his knowledge with humor to educate the public. What did Shakespeare say when he hiked to the bottom of the Grand Canyon? "A horse, a horse, my kingdom for a horse!" Stew was recognized as being a most unusual and loving person.

When he retired, he bought a house in Sedona, Arizona. He filled it with native-American and western art and two big dogs. Isis was a lady, calm and delicate. Gandhi was the biggest, strongest, most active, lovable dog on the planet. Gandhi was ghost-white, with a hard, square head. He would sit in the passenger seat of Stew's stinky, dog-hair covered Mini-Cooper. Stew thought it was funny when people thought Gandhi was a human sitting in the front seat. Dog-slobber covered every inch of the windows. It made it difficult to create a peep hole.

Stew had been incredibly strong in his youth, but no longer. Keeping Gandhi under control on a leash was getting to be a problem. While walking Gandhi, a rabbit bolted and so did Gandhi. Stew did not let go of the leash quickly enough. Gandhi was so strong that he dragged Stew along the walk until he hit the mail box. It resulted in a wound to his arm that required many stiches to repair.

But Stew loved that dog. He would not give up walking him. One evening, at dusk, they walked the road through the woods near his home. They turned when they heard an animal behind them. An elk in rut looked at them, wide-eyed and menacing. They were being threatened. The huge elk stood with his front legs splayed and he lowered his head. He began to sharpen his multi-pointed rack of antlers on the road. The elk swiped his horns to the right on the roadway, sharpening each tine. The heavy muscles in his neck then swiped the horns left on the gritty pavement. One could all but see sparks fly in the dusk. This was their last warning and the stag charged.

Stew dropped Gandhi's leash and the dog leaped the ditch and escaped into the pines. Stew headed to the opposite side of the road. That way, the elk could not chase the both of them. Stew bolted into the pines and hid in trees that were growing more closely together. That would keep the elk from charging Stew if he could not get his antlers between the trees. Stew waited until the elk moved away. When he could no longer see or hear the elk, he cautiously exited the woods. He quietly walked to the road and listened for the clip of elk hooves or the snort of his breath. Stew also listened for the sound of Gandhi's howl. That would mean that Gandhi had caught his leash on an obstruction and was struggling to be free. The elk might have gone after him. Stew did not hear the dog.

Stew walked home where Gandhi greeted him with his leash dragging and his tail between his legs. He seemed to apologize and say, "I am so sorry. I did not mean to desert you. Are you okay?"

Moonshine in the Moonlight

Death Valley National Park in California is indescribable, like no other. It leaves indelible memories of thick,white salt flats that are blinding in the brilliant sunshine. There are snow-capped mountains, sand dunes, canyons, flowers and ancient one-inch pupfish. I had not expected these beautiful things, but I had never expected a moonlight ride in the desert on the back of a mule.

A fellow Smithsonian Tour traveler had seen the moonlight ride poster on the hotel desk. It offered a guided horse ride into the Death Valley desert at night. This woman on the tour was beautiful with curly, full, chestnut colored hair. She went out of her way to prove she was unrestrained, wild. How could she not be with a name like Misty Carlucci? She ordered a bottle of expensive Italian wine for herself with each evening meal. She laughed often and loudly.

I signed up for the ride to go with this crazy lady. We were missing a filet supper for this. We arrived at the ranch inside the park where she immediately, and openly, tormented the young, handsome wranglers with her "suggestiveness." Pretty, crazy and bawdy.

There were seven of us, all women who had signed up for the ride. We were assigned horses, but I was last. They offered to me, Moonshine, a mule. I jumped at the opportunity. He was huge, black, and long legged. His head was enormous. The seat of the saddle was two feet above my head as I stood next to him. Wranglers provided wooden stairs for me to climb into the saddle. They shortened my stirrups three times, to the shortest notch, to accommodate my petite legs. If I were to fell off, if I survived, I would never be able to climb back onto him without a boost. As I sat on Moonshine, I observed a new perspective. I looked down on the horses with their riders and gloated, "So this is what it is like to feel big." I grinned and looked down from lofty heights..

The line of horses and riders left the corral just as the sun set. The last directions I heard were, "Don't forget, mules have a mind of their own. It takes a strong rider to pull their heads up to keep them from feeding along the way." Somehow, I had "forgotten" what I had never known.

On the trail, I learned that the mule's name, Moonshine, had nothing to do with the moon. He acted like a cocky, obstreperous drunk. Hence his name. He was independent and smart. Wranglers will tell you that horses will scatter in fright but mules will face their enemies. Mules will line up and lean hard into a corral fence to face an advancing grizzly bear. Moonshine had stopped twice to stare down a white jackrabbit to see if it were a threat. The jackrabbit had been lost to me in the white, glowing sand. The horses appeared to be unaware of it. It was good that Moonshine and I were at the end of the line of horses. With our stops, we did not slow down the other riders.

The gait of my mule was smooth. The saddle was comfortable, and surely, for the first time in my life, the ride was painless. This was the most enjoyable "horseback" ride of my life. However, my shoulders could feel that they might be sore by the time the ride was over. Moonshine's huge head needed to be pulled out of every mesquite hummock we passed. I would pull the reins as he tore a mouthful out of the heart of each tough plant.

I caught a glimpse of Misty. She had placed her horse's reins across the saddle. Her chestnut hair glowed in the moonlight. She was riding with such pleasure. She raised her smiling face and extended her hands out to the sides, basking in a shower of moon rays.

The evening was magical. Venus shone ahead of us to the southwest and the nearly full moon was high in the sky. The moon's brilliance washed all stars from the sky. The evening was warm with a calming breeze. The moonshine in the dry air lit the salt laden desert sand and filled the blue night with ambient light. The salty dust in the air rose eerily above the trail like cold fog over a warm stream.

Suddenly, from the dust, I had to sneeze. I knew I could not cover my mouth without a third hand so I grabbed the reins tightly to keep control of Moonshine. Then, trying not to sneeze, I exploded like a constricted canon. Moonshine shot off the trail and into the desert sands. The horses stopped and looked. The riders looked my way to see what the ruckus was and what the exploding noise had been. The lead wrangler wheeled to see if I needed to be rescued. I pulled on the reins as though I knew what I was doing and Moonshine, with his ears up like SETI antennae, stopped. I had stopped this freight-train fiasco. I had not been bucked off. I was so proud of myself that I sat in the saddle wearing a stupid grin. I had commanded a runaway mule. Bucket list! Check!

Moonshine chose a new place in line, and the ride continued. It became "girls' night out." We were nine women, including the guides. One was a wrangler, our leader. In her regular job, she packed mules for the national parks. It was March 8, 2017, International Women's Day. We took one day and celebrated us. We joked that the men had the rest of the year.

We were a short distance from the corral, the end of the ride, when a pack of coyotes howled. Each individual high-pitched coyote voice was clear in the dry air. One thinks of coyotes "howling in the distance," but these were so close, we felt their presence. It was a salute to us, for our sense of adventure, our accomplishments as women, our joy to the ride in their desert home.

Inside the corral, we did not want to dismount and give up our animals, but nothing gold can stay. I swung my leg over the saddle, grabbed the pommel, and removed my left foot from the stirrup. Dangling from the pommel, I lowered myself and then dropped the last three feet to the dusty ground. It had been Moonshine in the moonlight. Neither will be forgotten.

Tiny Child

I sat alone in a canvas chair at the top of the hill where it was slightly cooler. It was intermission to the annual Fourth of July "Salute to America" held at Greenfield Village in Dearborn. It was dusk, but I tried to read my book.

A tiny girl dropped softly onto her knees at the side of my chair. She did not face me. She studied her little silhouetted fingers and she spoke in a voice from Heaven. "Are you drinking your water?"

I was startled but I managed to realize what she was asking me. I spoke softly yet seriously, "Yes, it is important to drink water in such hot weather." She rose like a phantom and walked away.

A woman with a lovely countenance appeared above me to my left. I could see half of her face in the lantern light that lit the walkway. She had to be a young grandmother. Her thick dark hair was tied in a ribbon. She bent toward me and said, "She likes you, or she never would have spoken to you." She turned and followed the tiny child.